The Greatest Gift

Reviews

Sean has been a thoughtful, helpful, and deeply appreciated resource for our family in working through generational wealth transfer issues and considerations. Fortunately for everyone, he and Jill have encapsulated their store of knowledge in *The Greatest Gift*.

Mark McLaughlin*
Former Chairman and CEO: Palo Alto Networks
Chair of the Board: Qualcomm

Sean and Jill are the perfect, well-suited pair to lead caring people through the perilous and opportunistic minefield of wealth transfer.

Lee Gilbert*
Fourth-generation Investor

My wife and I have used these principles to successfully transfer family wealth to the next generation. We are grateful for the blessing this has been to our growing family.

Thomas A. Whiteman, PhD*
Author & Founder: Life Management, Inc.

Investment Advisory Services are offered through Valley Forge Investment Consultants, Inc. and VFPE Advisors, LLC, (together "Valley Forge"). The individuals indicated with an asterisk (*) are clients of Valley Forge and were not paid for their review of this book. Individuals marked with a double asterisk (**) are not clients of Valley Forge and were not paid for their review of this book.

The money game is tricky. Pitfalls abound, and that's true even when the family is fully intact. After a "repose," everything gets exponentially more difficult for the family. That's why a navigator is essential and, as a team, that's what Sean and Jill have produced—a navigation tool that should be held close as transitions evolve with relationships intact.

James G. & Jeanne Petrucci*
Founders: J.G. Petrucci, Co., Inc. & Living Plate Rx

It's amazing how so many successful people can share wealth and philosophical beliefs with their attorney, financial advisors, and business associates but neglect or for some reason can't or won't share them with family. *The Greatest Gift* provides practical steps to overcome this challenge.

Susan Garber Brown & Edward S. Brown*
Founders: Edward S. Brown Group

When answering questions, experience matters. This must-read book brings you the experience to manage your greatest gift.

Stephen A. Tullman*
Founder: Nexstone Innovation
Biotech Entrepreneur

I have known Sean and Jill for almost 30 years. Sean has done a great job with the estate plan for our family and helped us achieve our philanthropic goals. The principles outlined in this book are critical

---

Investment Advisory Services are offered through Valley Forge Investment Consultants, Inc. and VFPE Advisors, LLC, (together "Valley Forge"). The individuals indicated with an asterisk (*) are clients of Valley Forge and were not paid for their review of this book. Individuals marked with a double asterisk (**) are not clients of Valley Forge and were not paid for their review of this book.

for families to find a balance between estate and tax planning, and sustaining family harmony. The stories are entertaining, relatable, and informative. This is a valuable resource for families who have sufficient means to fund their own retirement and can now focus on efficient wealth transfer and family relationships.

Donald J. Steiner*
Founder: Webster Equity Partners

As Sean and Jill so deftly describe in this book, wealth and emotions are two sides of the same coin. Routinely, as Sean relates through his vast experience with ultrahigh-net-worth individuals, too often it is the potential emotional pitfalls of wealth transfer that often get neglected in the planning process.

This is a must-read for parents who want to leave a legacy that not only reflects the fruits of their labor, but, in equal measure, the values that sustained them and their families. For heirs, *The Greatest Gift* provides valuable lessons on how to best steward their good fortune and honor their benefactors in the process.

Brint Detwiler**
Founder and President: Barnstone Advisors

The Greatest Gift provides a practical guide to the human and psychological aspects of estate planning.

Michael C. McBratnie, Esq.**
Former Chair of Taxation
Partner: Fox Rothschild

Investment Advisory Services are offered through Valley Forge Investment Consultants, Inc. and VFPE Advisors, LLC, (together "Valley Forge"). The individuals indicated with an asterisk (*) are clients of Valley Forge and were not paid for their review of this book. Individuals marked with a double asterisk (**) are not clients of Valley Forge and were not paid for their review of this book.

Sean's vast knowledge of wealth management has been a tremendous support for our family over the years, and Jill's expertise as a psychological counselor provides a compassionate voice to Sean's approach. Their synergistic efforts make *The Greatest Gift* an invaluable resource that contains ready-to-implement principles to guide everyone through the wealth transfer process with practicality and empathy.

Partha & Divya Mukherjee*
Founder: AVS, Inc. & Health Coach

Sean and Jill understand the complexities that factor into successful wealth transfer. *The Greatest Gift* is a helpful resource for families wanting talk about what really matters.

Tina Lovejoy **
Founder: Frameworks Facilitation LLC

Meryl and I had a goal of helping our children but also creating self-confident and motivated individuals who can lead successful independent lives. We appreciate having the help of Sean who helps us and others with the issues of wealth transfer and hope this book written by Jill and Sean is helpful to you and your family.

Chuck Witmer*
Co-managing member
Eagle Value Partners

Investment Advisory Services are offered through Valley Forge Investment Consultants, Inc. and VFPE Advisors, LLC, (together "Valley Forge"). The individuals indicated with an asterisk (*) are clients of Valley Forge and were not paid for their review of this book. Individuals marked with a double asterisk (**) are not clients of Valley Forge and were not paid for their review of this book.

The Greatest Gift

9 Principles for the Transfer of Your Legacy along with Your Wealth

Sean Maher *and* Jill Maher

NEW YORK
LONDON • NASHVILLE • MELBOURNE • VANCOUVER

The Greatest Gift
9 Principles for the Transfer of Your Legacy along with Your Wealth

© 2025 Sean Maher, Jill Maher

All rights reserved. No portion of this book may be reproduced, stored in a retrieval system, or transmitted in any form or by any means—electronic, mechanical, photocopy, recording, scanning, or other—except for brief quotations in critical reviews or articles, without the prior written permission of the publisher.

Published in New York, New York, by Morgan James Publishing. Morgan James is a trademark of Morgan James, LLC. www.MorganJamesPublishing.com

Proudly distributed by Publishers Group West®

Morgan James BOGO™

A **FREE** ebook edition is available for you or a friend with the purchase of this print book.

CLEARLY SIGN YOUR NAME ABOVE

Instructions to claim your free ebook edition:
1. Visit MorganJamesBOGO.com
2. Sign your name CLEARLY in the space above
3. Complete the form and submit a photo of this entire page
4. You or your friend can download the ebook to your preferred device

ISBN 9781636985084 paperback
ISBN 9781636985107 ebook
ISBN 9781636985091 hardcover
Library of Congress Control Number: 2024938837

Cover and Interior Design by:
Chris Treccani
www.3dogcreative.net

Cover image by:
Cameron Maher
www.cameronmaher.com

Morgan James PUBLISHING Builds with... Habitat for Humanity Peninsula and Greater Williamsburg

Morgan James is a proud partner of Habitat for Humanity Peninsula and Greater Williamsburg. Partners in building since 2006.

Get involved today! Visit: www.morgan-james-publishing.com/giving-back

Dedication

Mom and Dad, thank you for modeling partnership for all of us. I cannot think of anyone more selfless.

Jill, I am blessed to have you as my life partner, coach, and loudest cheerleader.

Zach, Ryan, and Kylie, I look forward to all that lies ahead for you and your future families.

Disclaimer

The names of individuals and families throughout this book have been changed to protect their privacy. While I have changed their names, I have incorporated real quotes that struck a chord with me.

Case Studies: This book contains real-life case studies and examples, whether from my work or stories I've been told by colleagues at events across the country. Unless the story is from publicly available data or involves my family, events have been modified, altered, or fictionalized to protect the privacy and identities of individuals involved. Any resemblances to actual persons, living or deceased, are purely coincidental.

Fictional Elements: In addition to changing names, I have also changed locations, events, timelines, and other details to protect the privacy and identities of individuals involved. I have exercised creative license to present engaging narratives while maintaining anonymity.

Confidentiality and Anonymity: I have taken great care to ensure that the identities, personal information, and sensitive details of individuals portrayed in the case studies have been sufficiently disguised or altered. However, it is possible that some similarities may exist between the fictionalized accounts and real-life events or persons. Any perceived similarities are unintentional.

Generalized Lessons: The primary purpose of including case studies in this book is to illustrate broader concepts, principles, or lessons rather than to provide an accurate and comprehensive account of specific individuals or situations.

Professional Advice: The information presented in this book is not legal, accounting, investment, tax, or mental health advice. It is not a substitute for professional guidance or expertise. It is essential to consult appropriate professionals or experts for specific advice related to legal, accounting, investment, tax, or mental health matters. The case studies are intended to provoke thought, but they should not be considered as authoritative or prescriptive.

Table of Contents

Foreword xvii
A Note from Sean xix
Introduction: Is this Book for You? xxvii

The 9 Principles for Successful Wealth Transfer
   1. Develop a Common Purpose 1
   2. Share Your Story 23
   3. Forge Traditions 41
   4. Define Roles 61
   5. Promote Humility 83
   6. Nurture Independence 103
   7. Encourage Giving 133
   8. Create a Safe Environment 155
   9. Overcommunicate 177
  10. Overview: The 9 Principles for Successful Wealth Transfer . 209

Postscript: A New House 217
About the Authors 221
Acknowledgments 223
So, What Now? 225

Foreword

It is with great pleasure and excitement that I present to you this foreword for the book on high-net-worth families and their plans for generational wealth transfer strategies.

The Greatest Gift delves into the intricate world of wealth management, exploring the strategies and considerations that affluent families have employed to preserve and transfer their wealth across generations.

In today's rapidly changing economic landscape, the importance of effective wealth transfer planning cannot be overstated. High-net-worth families face unique challenges and opportunities when it comes to managing their wealth and ensuring its longevity. This book aims to provide valuable insights and practical guidance to help navigate this complex terrain.

Within these pages, you will find a comprehensive exploration of various wealth transfer strategies, including estate planning, trust structures, charitable giving, and family governance. The authors have meticulously researched and compiled *9 Principles for Successful Wealth Transfer*, drawing from their extensive experience in working with affluent families as their trusted advisors.

One of the key themes that resonates throughout this book is the importance of taking a holistic approach to wealth transfer. It goes beyond the mere financial aspects and delves into the dynamics of family relationships, communication, and values.

The authors emphasize the significance of open and transparent discussions within the family, fostering a shared vision and a sense of purpose for the wealth being transferred.

Whether you are an individual seeking guidance on preserving your wealth for future generations, a family member involved in wealth transfer discussions, or a professional advisor serving affluent families, this book is a valuable resource that will deepen your understanding and enhance your ability to navigate the complexities of generational wealth transfer.

I encourage you to embark on this journey of discovery and empowerment as you delve into the pages of this insightful book. May it inspire you to contemplate your own wealth transfer strategies and ignite meaningful conversations within your family, ultimately paving the way for a lasting legacy of prosperity and impact.

Thomas L. duPont

A Note from Sean

"That's not how *I* remember it . . ."

The death of a parent can be like pulling the pin on a grenade. The parent dies and the family explodes into turmoil, into an uncivil war all because of different interpretations of what mom or dad wanted regarding their estate.

In fact, having to say, **"Mom (or Dad) would have wanted . . ."** is the worst phrase for any heir to utter.

It doesn't have to be this way, though.

No matter the size of your estate, if you plan well and communicate clearly, you can avoid things getting contentious after your passing.

Do you think your family is different or immune to conflict after you are gone? Think again.

In my almost 30 years as a financial consultant, I've witnessed things going in one of two directions when it comes to the transfer of wealth.

I've seen things go great—those left behind continuing the legacy of the patriarch or matriarch. Sadly, I've also seen things go so poorly that siblings are no longer on speaking terms. Some even end up in court.

That's why I wrote this book. If you're in the camp of those who wish for a smooth transfer of wealth not only *after* your passing but starting *now*, I'll show you what you can do.

I'll also show you where the land mines are, which pitfalls you can avoid, and what challenges to overcome so your heirs can live in harmony and enjoy the fruits of your hard work.

There's too much at stake to simply *hope* things go well once you're no longer around. Instead, I'll provide you with some principles you can apply starting today so you can preserve your legacy.

||||||||||||

Like many families, our family adopted a "COVID puppy" during the lockdowns of 2020. Apollo, a German shepherd, was a pleasant distraction for our family through that period and continues to be the inspiration (or demand) for my wife, Jill, and me to take nightly walks. Now weighing in at a lean 95 pounds, Apollo is more of a beast than a puppy!

During our walks, it is common for Jill and me to talk about the principles from this book. While my insights come from a financial angle, Jill's are from her expertise as a clinical mental health counselor.

On our walks, I share my perspective about something I observed in conversation with a family and their wealth, and Jill looks at it from a relational and emotions-centered lens. Apollo listens in and keeps us walking along.

In the pages that follow, Jill and I have integrated our expertise because we know that money is important, but so are the relationships with and among your family. You'll want to preserve both.

At the end of each chapter, Jill will share her insights so you can understand the tension and avoid relational land mines. She will provide insights into how emotions drive many of the negative behaviors that lead to family conflict and provide you with practical steps to defuse such tension as well as additional resources you can refer to.

I have always admired Jill's ability to handle difficult questions with simple, relevant insights, and I hope those will be a big help as you embark on the next steps of preparing your heirs for a smooth transition after you are gone.

||||||||||||

Over the years, I've worked with more than 300 families as a financial planner. And based on actual cases I've dealt with—camouflaged for privacy—I'll show you what could be true for your family if you were to apply the principles we have developed. And sadly, I'll give you a glimpse of what has happened where folks simply hoped for the best.

If you leverage the principles outlined in this book, your heirs will never have to use "Mom and Dad would have wanted . . ." to sway an argument or manipulate others.

If you communicate clearly, concisely, and directly, you'll leave no room for uncertainty, assumptions, and ambiguity. No room for conflict. No place for grief to turn to greed.

Instead, your family will know *exactly* what you want to happen when you're no longer around. And uniting them around a common goal starts right *now*.

||||||||||||

A successful transfer of wealth balances efficiency and family harmony.

Everyone wants to pay the least amount of frictional costs like taxes and probate expenses at death, and plan well for creditor protection and special needs. Unfortunately, many families stop at the point of efficiency. They never address the emotional and less tangible parts of leaving an inheritance.

To make things worse, they wait until death to start dealing with the transfer of wealth. Little do they know there are things they can do *now* to help to facilitate the outcomes and desires they want for their wealth.

Years ago, I personally experienced what a successful transfer of wealth can look like. It has fueled my passion for helping others do the same.

Where It All Started

As kids, our family would count down the days till "summer camp," which consisted of a few days at our Uncle George and Aunt Karen's home in Pennsylvania. (Aunt Karen is my dad's sister.)

We'd make the 90-minute drive from our home in southern New Jersey across the Delaware River, through downtown Philadelphia, and, eventually, just to the other side of the Valley Forge National Historic Park.

Most mornings at the Beyers's home, we woke up to the smell of pancakes and bacon. After a hearty breakfast, all eight cousins would play capture the flag, go to a water park, play Intellivision, or make up "shows" we'd later perform to the adults.

Fast forward to 1996. I was working as the head of reservations at a hotel in Georgia—a job that came with more stress than I cared to live with for the rest of my career. I had no idea what I was getting into when at a young age I decided on a career in hospitality and enrolled at Cornell's Hotel School.

I have to say, those early years taught me a lot about being customer focused. But after just a couple of years in the hotel business, I was burned out and thought it would be a great idea to start a marketing company. I asked Uncle George to be my first investor. After all, he had built a thriving financial services company from scratch.

Oh, my ignorance! I had no business plan and no experience. But rather than ridicule me, my uncle invited me to interview for a position at the financial-services company he and my Aunt Karen had started in 1967. My brother Mike had already been working at Valley Forge for four years by that time.

Uncle George had trained as a life insurance agent in Chicago, but he and his wife wanted to live closer to their childhood homes in Philadelphia. So, after a few short years in the Midwest and with the unwavering support and sacrifice of Aunt Karen, he took the leap of faith to move back east and start Valley Forge Financial Group, Inc. (My aunt fondly refers to those early years of the business as their "rice and beans" years.)

I passed the interview, but my uncle had a few requirements: I was to call him by his first name, and I had to be prepared to work harder than everyone else.

Everyone knew I was his nephew even though our last names didn't match. And while it took some getting used to calling my uncle by his first name, I had no qualms working hard. I was used to it, and I was eager.

At the time, George was in his late 50s and at the peak of his career. He took me under his wing and personally trained me, something I still consider an incredible honor. Neither of us knew I would be his final trainee.

One of many disciplines George instilled in me was careful recordkeeping.

Because of him, I can tell you to this day precisely how many families I've worked with, that I've clocked 5,500 workdays, and I've had 8,000 in-person meetings with clients do date.

In 1998, two years after starting my career in financial services, George organized a family investment partnership—an investment club, if you will. The partnership included George and Karen, their daughters, Colleen and Kathleen, and my brother Mike and me.

George *loved* investing, and he and Karen wanted to share his passion and use the investment club to educate the four of us—all in our twenties when it started and new to the world of direct stock investing.

The partnership would be our opportunity to experiment and make mistakes—all with George's mentorship and wisdom as our safety net.

At first, it gave us a forum to discuss investments. But over time, it fostered mutual respect, a sense of belonging, worthiness, and capability. It also allowed us to establish positions within the family structure.

What none of us realized at the time was that by assembling our group, George was modeling what it looks like to initiate a smooth transfer of wealth.

Just a year after George started the partnership, he was diagnosed with Parkinson's disease. This led to him accelerating the transfer of his long-term client relationships, opening the door for my colleagues and me to take lead on relationships where George had been providing financial guidance for more than 30 years.

For me, this was a tremendous opportunity to launch into high-net-worth and ultrahigh-net-worth client consulting, and for those clients to refer similar families to me.

Fourteen years later, in 2011, when George passed away due to complications from Parkinson's, we were all terribly sad, but there was no tension among those of us who inherited his clients and the family business.

We knew *exactly* what George wanted.

George set the blueprint for many of the principles of this book. He wasn't explicit with a "plan," but the patterns he set forth are strikingly similar to patterns I observed interviewing second- and third-generation families who preserved their family relationships through the wealth-transfer process.

⁝⁝⁝⁝⁝⁝⁝⁝⁝⁝⁝

There are many emotions involved when a loved one passes. An inheritance can exacerbate those, causing the ones who stand to benefit from the estate—or not—to behave in ways they may have never seen coming.

Like what George unknowingly did for us, my goal is to inspire your family to avoid the lasting distress that can be created by an inheritance.

With each of the principles, I'll share stories that will contrast two emotions: one *constructive* and one *destructive*. And while even the healthiest among us might tip toward the destructive following the death of a loved one, the tools I'll be offering will help encourage the constructive emotions.

These stories aren't shared for sensationalism. I have seen very positive and inspiring transitions, and conversely, some very disturbing and heartbreaking transitions of wealth. By sharing these stories and practical tools, I hope to offer you examples from which you can learn.

By the end of this book, you will know the principles and accumulate the inspiration to give your heirs *the greatest gift*.

Introduction
Is this Book for You?

This book is for anyone who values *relational wealth* as much as they value *financial wealth*.

It's for *you*—parents, aunts and uncles, grandparents, or anyone who envisions their heirs thriving and living in harmony someday after they are gone—to put to good use the resources you have worked hard to create.

This book is also for you as an inheritor, a current or future beneficiary of a family with enough wealth and possessions to understand the potential pitfalls thereof and who wish to be a catalyst for proactive conversation with your benefactors, your siblings, cousins, or anyone else who might share in the inheritance.

Wealth. Don't let that word get in the way of reading this book. Defining wealth, net worth, and assets is relative to each person's perspective.

While my professional experience is working with high- and ultrahigh-net-worth families, **the concepts outlined in this book are universal.** The principles are the same whether the future inheritance is $100,000 or $100,000,000.

The same concepts apply even if the only asset you'll bequeath to someone else is your home. Have you decided how your home will be left to your heirs? Do you have a plan? Do your inheritors know what the plan is?

It's not about the size of your estate; it's about principles.

We all tend to count our zeros, especially the number of zeros in our net worth. But zeros can be a multiplier for emotions when it comes to inheritance. I have observed that the more zeros someone has, the more money they have, the more magnified emotions tend to become—not only during their time on earth but often even more once they've passed.

Everyone knows a story of an inheritance gone wrong. I'm sure you know one too. Maybe you've even experienced it yourself. Or perhaps you simply observed it, maybe through a friend or family members. It may even be a story passed down in your family of a time when someone was cheated out of their rightful share to a family inheritance or a family heirloom and they're still bitter about it.

The media and entertainment industry certainly loves this topic, so much so that many movies are written around this theme. The list includes *The Weekend Murders* (1970, comedic horror), *Brewster's Millions* (1985, comedy), *Rain Man* (1988, drama), *The Bachelor* (1999, romantic comedy) *The Descendants* (2011, tragicomedy), *Knives Out* (2019, crime mystery), and *Inheritance* (2020, thriller)—to name but a few.

TV shows that touch on this theme, whether at the core of the show or just as a reference in an episode or two, include the hit HBO show *Succession* (2018–2023), and *Downton Abbey* (2010–2015), not to mention a multitude of true-crime shows.

This book ensures your family will not be the subject of a *Dateline* episode or the next Hollywood disaster blockbuster.

Consider this an easy preventive maintenance guide so your children aren't at war with each other—or worse—after you die.

The 9 Principles for Successful Wealth Transfer

1

Develop a Common Purpose

Future shock is the shattering stress and disorientation that we induce in individuals by subjecting them to too much change in too short a time.
~Alvin Toffler

When George established the family investment partnership, he wanted all of us—George, Karen, Colleen, Kathleen, and Mike and me—to make collective investment decisions. Rather than giving us company profits each year and encouraging us to invest these individually, we worked together to decide how to invest the funds.

George was a student of value investing and was intent on training us to be the same. So, before we risked making poor investment choices, his first assignment to us

Principle 1:
Develop a Common Purpose
Destructive Emotion:
Jealousy
Constructive Emotion:
Connection
Proposition:
Engagement is essential.

1

was to read *Buffettology*.[1] The book explains the techniques that made Warren Buffett the world's most famous investor.

Following the key elements of analysis recommended in *Buffettology* and using tools like Morningstar—an investment research platform, complete with analyst commentary and a company rating system for almost every publicly traded stock in the US stock markets—we would screen stocks that might be worth buying.

We all had to agree on what we'd invest in. And we would put the money to work as if we were running Berkshire Hathaway just like Warren Buffet.

Not all our stock picks were winners, of course, but it gave us a common purpose—to maximize the return on our investments. After all, we were risking our own profits!

Buffettology gave us a model to follow, and the mix of ideas and diverse perspectives from within our family partnership helped keep us on target toward our goals. It also made our two-hour monthly meetings go by in a flash. (Later, we shifted to quarterly meetings.)

Picture the six of us, gathered around the same dining room table from our magical childhood summer visits, with papers everywhere and lots of spreadsheets. Midway through, Karen would go get one of her famous cherry pies from the oven to "keep up our energy."

Early on, the meetings were led by George. The rest of us were all just trying to keep up and contribute if we could. Over time, we all settled into our roles, and George simply took on the role as mentor.

---

1   Mary Buffett & David Clark. 1999. *Buffettology: The Previously Unexplained Techniques That Have Made Warren Buffett the World's Most Famous Investor.* Scribner.

Mike soon became our leader. He organized the meeting schedule, kept thorough notes, and held us accountable to the follow-up items from each meeting.

My role became that of analyst. I prepared our projected return model for each company, compared insights to the teachings from *Buffettology*, and found reasons why *not* to invest in companies. This led to the others referring to me as "Mr. Cynical."

Colleen became our chief reason officer. She was the one who always brought decisions back to asking, "Why are we doing this? Does it make sense for the partnership?"

As the youngest and the hippest in our group—in touch with new products on the market and what was popular—Kathleen naturally was our head of new ideas. She always had good companies to consider for investment.

Karen became the ethics enforcer. She looked at nonfinancial components—environmental, social, or governance concerns. There were several instances where an investment looked good on paper, but Karen's insights led to it being overruled.

As for accounting and tax preparation, quarterly administration, and legal work, we relied on outside resources.

Having a reason to meet quarterly to discuss investment performance, new investment ideas, and the ongoing administration of the family partnership became a true bond and continues to provide us meaningful purpose to this day.

The nature of *Buffettology* and investing together was to constantly challenge each person's ideas. We learned how to respectfully disagree and speak our minds about investment decisions. Conflicts were rare, but the debates were frequent. Each of us had to defend our position and listen and respect the views of the others.

For example, when I suggested a certain pharmaceutical company as an investment, Colleen strongly disagreed. Her training and occupation as a veterinarian made her aware and sensitive to animal-testing practices. We debated the issue and after research that verified Colleen's concerns, I was convinced that the company's repeated negative behavior did not outweigh the possible economic gains we could get from the investment.

Of course, throughout these meetings, we also kept close personal ties and exchanged regular updates about family and non-business interests.

Looking back, I suspect George intuitively knew how important this investment partnership would become to all of us, how it would give us confidence in our abilities and pride in our decision-making, and most of all, that it would deepen our relationships.

The meetings also gave us a common purpose.

George and Karen were a beautiful example of how to successfully communicate their vision. I am not sure if they created the investment club for this reason, but it has certainly served this purpose.

During George's 10-year battle with Parkinson's and for eight years after his death, Karen, our cousins, Mike, and I served together on the board of directors of Valley Forge. We shared the profits of the business, contributed the profits to our family investment partnership, and continued holding quarterly meetings. Plus, we stayed in communication about the strategies, successes, and failures of our growing financial-services business.

In 2019, after almost three years of careful consideration and regular communication, Mike and I led the buyout of founder's stock from Karen and our cousins Colleen and Kathleen who had chosen to follow career paths that took them to professions outside of financial services.

George and Karen had made it clear that family harmony between Mike, me, and our cousins was paramount. Hence, our guiding principle for the buyout was that family harmony had to come first. Even in the buyout, none of us were willing to sacrifice our deep family relationship—whatever the cost, and however long it would take.

I can only imagine the difficult emotions my aunt and cousins felt around the sale of their family business. The pride and legacy of the business George created cannot be expressed in dollar amounts.

But the family investment partnership had given us a common purpose that had put into motion a seamless transfer.

The Value of Developing a Common Purpose

Receiving an inheritance can lead to *a lot* of change. And the larger the bequest, the more change—sometimes too much in too short a time. These changes can create conflict and, in the worst case, alienation.

No matter the dollar amount, **the best way to equip family members for the shock of inheritance is to provide them with a common purpose.** Think of a common purpose as a series of long-term shared goals that bind individuals together through teamwork, engagement, and reinforcement.

As parents, for example, we have a common purpose of tending to our children's every need while we raise them.

Similarly, companies strive to create a common purpose consistent with their company mission statement and its core values. At my company, when we organize team-building days, we seek experiences that bond us—say, an escape room or a challenging ropes course. And for years afterward, we reinforce the teamwork and engagement brought by those experiences, remembering how they helped us accomplish extraordinary tasks. They helped reinforce our common purpose of having a healthy and cohesive work environment.

A common purpose can take many forms. No matter the form, though, having a common purpose serves as the training ground for personal interaction and builds the solid foundation for functional, cooperative behavior. In families it creates respect, a sense of belonging, a sense of worthiness and capability, and establishes position within the family structure.

Having a common purpose also helps reinforce a common vision—an ideal or series of ideals toward a future image. When a group shares a common vision, they desire the same outcomes and are willing to work hard and make sacrifices toward that future state. A **common vision** is often the *inspiration* for a common purpose.

As parents pursue the common purpose of tending to their children's every need, they do so with the common vision of the children growing into well-adjusted, productive members of society.

Without having a common vision, family groups are left disoriented. This is a major source of conflict. **Having a clear vision helps with orientation**, providing an internal compass that helps everyone make decisions when they don't quite know which way to turn.

Again, in parenting, when a child isn't accepted to their first-choice college or picked for the sports team, rather than being stuck in despair, parents can reflect on their common purpose (tend to children's needs) and vision (creating productive members of society) to orient them and inform their response to what the child needs and what the best next step is to guide their next move.

No matter your net worth, having a common purpose can bring your family closer together. First, identify interests that everyone has in common, then discern the purpose behind it, and have consistent and regular get-togethers that center around this purpose.

If everyone has an interest in investing, consider creating an investment club where you and your family meet four times a year to discuss investing principles and topics. The purpose is to grow everyone's savings.

If investing doesn't appeal to you, find something else that intentionally brings you together as a family. The list of options is endless: fishing, supporting your favorite sports team, crafting, baking, and volunteering, whether to build a home through a non-profit such as Habitat for Humanity, picking a local park or beach to clean up as a family, or helping communities near yours during times of natural disasters.

Whatever you pick, let it be something that connects you as a family around a common purpose. Coupling these activities with a great meal and camaraderie creates the desire for everyone to show up.

But even something like working together to care for grandparents, or siblings partnering in caring for aging parents can become an opportunity that unites a family. While carefully coordinated, organized, and intentional care is not easy, it can also be an example of selflessness and compassion and serve as inspiration for your children on what common purpose can look like.

Finding a Common Purpose by Establishing Family Partnerships and Private Foundations

For high-net-worth families, my interviews with inheritors and advisers alike revealed that the use of family partnerships and private foundations are excellent ways to create a common purpose.

Partnerships and foundations provide the structure and forum necessary to create healthy engagement. They allow for the gradual involvement of next-generation participants, which I've observed to be a pathway to harmony.

Family partnerships can take many forms. In its simplest form, a partnership may be the structured, deliberate involvement of the next generation in the management of, say, a family vacation home. In its more complicated form, it may be a legal structure like an **LLC** (a limited liability company) or a **limited partnership**.

Whatever form it takes, a family partnership ideally should have regularly scheduled meetings, a shared common purpose and vision, and a structure for decision-making.

It is not necessary for the family partnership to give control to the younger generation—whether those are family members in their 20s or their 50s. What's most important is simply that the younger generation is involved in the conversation, and possibly, the management of assets.

As for **private foundations**, those are legally formed as a **trust** or a **corporation**. These are tax-exempt entities, and to qualify as such, they have very strict recordkeeping and reporting requirements.

Like with LLCs and partnerships, foundations should have regularly scheduled meetings, a shared common purpose and vision, and a structure for decision-making.

Families that do not have enough to form a foundation can replicate a private foundation with their annual charitable giving or by using a **donor-advised fund**, an IRS-recognized separate account that is maintained to receive charitable donations. The fund is not an operating charity, but more of a holding account.

With donor-advised funds, a donor can make a contribution today and take the tax benefits immediately while reserving the right to recommend the ultimate distribution to a charity or charities at a later date. This technique has become so popular that donor-advised funds have become some of the largest charitable funds in the world.

Family Foundations: A Case Study

Establishing family partnerships and foundations serves to foster mutual respect, a sense of belonging, a sense of worthiness and capability, and position within the family structure. Best of all, they underscore the family's common purpose.

To learn more about family foundations, I interviewed Gloria Hughes. She heads up the family office—an office that handles the administration and communication around the family wealth—for the Robinsons, one of the wealthiest families in the USA.[2]

Hughes identified the use of a private foundation as the single most important factor in maintaining peace and harmony through the generations. She explained that the Robinson Foundation has quarterly meetings to which everyone in the family is invited—from newborns to the oldest members of the family.

The inclusivity and life lessons that are taught through involvement in these meetings are invaluable. By the time the Robinson children become adults and are made aware of their inheritance, they are already well versed in the following areas:

---

[2] Note that each family office is different, often taking cues and philosophy from its founders. Some family offices handle the administration and communication about family wealth. Others have many employees who are tasked with supporting the family in every way possible; legal services, tax compliance, wealth management, security, technology support, travel coordination, risk mitigation, property management, and bill paying. In other cases, a family office might be just one person who serves as more of an executive assistant—coordinating professionals who provide the various services for the family.

- **Vision:** The foundation is the giving arm of the family. It represents their family's mission to have a positive influence in the world. As such, the foundation is an offshoot of the family. Discussions during meetings naturally reinforce the family's values and vision and provide repeated exposure.
- **Structure:** Regularly scheduled meetings require structure. Participants are expected to keep a calendar, be on time, be presentable, and contribute.
- **Healthy Debate and Disagreement:** Adults at the foundation meetings model courteous, professional behavior. Disagreements are expected, and debates are encouraged. From an early age, family members learn the proper way to deal with conflict. This is important, especially with family and as it pertains to money.
- **Fiscal Discipline and Budgeting:** Every year, the foundation is required to give a certain amount of money. The foundation also has expenses for legal and accounting services. Each year, the family creates and approves a budget. At every meeting, they do a review of the foundation's financials and their performance to budget. The board of the foundation legally manages the family trust, and they understand their role as stewards of the family assets.
- **Money Management:** Imagine hearing the phrases "asset allocation" and "modern portfolio theory" as a five-year-old! By the time beneficiaries reach adulthood, these phrases are ingrained, and this allows them to apply these money-management principles once they are leaders of the foundation as well as regarding their personal wealth.
- **Robert's Rules of Order:** The foundation meetings use the famous Robert's Rules, designed "to assist an assembly

to accomplish the work for which it is designed." Early exposure to Robert's Rules gives children and young adults a predictable format for meetings that they can eventually apply in future non-profit involvement and in running their own family meetings someday. They can also utilize the principles in their future career.

- **The Role of Advisors:** The foundation uses outside, paid advisors for legal matters, tax preparation and compliance, and money management. Understanding the need for content experts and professional help, where necessary, is an important life skill. Managing the advisory team may be challenging at times, but observing the hiring and firing process is educational.
- **Confidentiality:** Deliberations about grants and important decisions made at the meetings are kept in the highest confidence. The children are taught at a very young age what can and cannot be shared publicly.

By exposing younger generations to detailed conversations on each of these topics, the family has empowered each generation with the tools it needs to successfully navigate the most common challenges and threats to family peace.

During our conversation, Hughes shared the contrast she had seen between working with the Robinsons and other affluent families who had not taken a similar inclusive approach to managing family assets.

By the time funds are distributed to them from the family trust, Robinson family inheritors are well prepared. They know how to budget and live within their means. They are generally more deliberate, aware, and disciplined with their spending, and they are knowledgeable about saving and money management.

Their perspectives on wealth have been shaped over time and rather than seeking to find the spending power of the assets, they view the assets as something to be preserved and managed.

Finding a Common Purpose in Bonding Over "Common Enemies"

No one likes to pay taxes. No one ever has. All the way back to Roman times, no one ever liked the tax collector.

Most meetings about estate planning focus on ways to shield family assets from as much estate and inheritance tax as possible. The Internal Revenue Service (IRS) of the United States government is *everyone's* common enemy. *But family members can also become a common enemy.*

I have observed families bonding over a difficult family member, or like with Nancy Clay in the story below, over their parents.

Nancy Clay's Absent Parents

Thomas and Nancy Clay were one of the first couples I interviewed for this book. I knew most of Nancy's origin story. Or so I thought.

The Clays had no hesitation when I called to tell them about the book and asked if they'd be willing to chat about some of the ideas I was exploring.

"Sounds fun," Thomas said. "Why don't you come to the beach? It's off season, and the weather is beautiful."

Later that week, I drove 90 minutes down to Rehoboth, Delaware.

Meeting Nancy, you would never know she is a fourth-generation heir to a family fortune created in the early days of the paper pulp industry. She and Thomas drive modest, American-made cars, and other than the fact their home is on the beach and has a spectacular view of the ocean, it is unassuming—just like Nancy's choice in clothing.

Nancy is a hugger and has a warm, magnanimous smile. If you're not comfortable with hugs, well, you just have to deal with it.

After a hug from Nancy and a handshake from Thomas, we settled in at the kitchen table with the ocean as our backdrop. It was one of those days the sun's rays were piercing the clouds and casting spotlights onto the water.

Nancy seemed comfortable and was very open to telling me everything. As we were visiting, I realized Nancy had probably only shared her family story with Thomas and a handful of other people. It was a relief for her to talk about it. Once in a while, Thomas would fill in details that may have been overlooked. He knew her story very well and was her emotional support.

Nancy grew up in the wealthiest neighborhood in Atlanta. Hers was the biggest house on the block, maybe in the entire city. She had a nursemaid—her nanny—from the day she was born, a laundress, a maid, and a butler. She saw her nanny more often than she saw her mother and father.

Nancy told me she remembers being consoled by her nanny one evening when she had a nightmare. Looking back, as a mother herself, she still harbors confusion about how her parents were comfortable with delegating night duty to a hired hand.

Nancy's mom survived her father by almost a year. I asked what it was like when her mom died, triggering the estate to distribute. I was expecting Nancy's response to be about arguments among her and her siblings about the silver and the fine furniture and artwork.

Turns out, none of them cared. They were united in their discontentment with their parents. "Our family home was not a happy place," Nancy bluntly admitted. "There was no sentimentality to the home itself or its contents."

Only one of her brothers cared about "the stuff." None of them even argued over their inheritance.

⸻

It became surprisingly clear after speaking with the Clays and others who were raised with wealth that having a common bond was an ingredient to family harmony—even if that bond was something negative.

For example, families often see taxes and creditors as enemies around which they unite. They would go to great lengths to protect family assets, even holding regular meetings focused solely on finding ways to protect their assets from these so-called enemies.

In many of my interviews, it was apparent that a third-party gatekeeper was often also viewed as a common adversary over which inheritors bonded. Complaints centered on having to ask these fiduciaries for distributions or loans from family trusts, and it led to family members bonding over their dislike of this common enemy.

Like the Clays, families with one or both parents serving as a common enemy created a source of bonding. Many siblings reacted by supporting each other in creating healthy family cultures for themselves.

While common enemies may bond inheritors negatively, having a common purpose serves as the solution to orienting children and grandchildren to the family vision and culture.

Without the deliberate effort of creating a common purpose, it is easy to see how inheritors can feel alienated rather than oriented toward a common vision.

The Role of Identifying Values in Finding a Common Purpose

Discerning your family purpose can be done through having a family mission statement. To write such a statement, though, it helps identifying first what you value.

1. Determine Your Family Values

This is a complex exercise, and it will take time. Brainstorm values around the table, then narrow it down to four or five that everyone agrees on as representing your family and its stakeholders.

(Some potential stakeholders include members of the immediate family, multiple generations—born and unborn—brothers and sisters of the parents, employees of the family company, and charities you support.)

Do not dictate what you believe your family values should be. Invite participation by making it clear that every person has an equal voice at the table, that their opinion matters, that they belong. Extend the opportunity for everyone to identify what *they* see as your family values and why these values are important to them. Be sure to have someone capture everyone's input.

Another way you can engage everyone is to give all family members a list of values to go through. Even more engaging is to print or purchase decks of cards with values printed on them. (Check out www.TheGreatestGiftBook.com for resources.)

Each person can go through the list or the deck and keep five values. At the end, ask every person to share the five values they picked and why they believe those represent your family.

Once you have a list of values, identify ones that were picked by multiple family members. As a family, discuss which five values everyone feels reflect the shared family values.

Consider having at least one value each that represents the body, mind, and spirit of the family stakeholders.

2. Define Your Values
Once you have identified your values, define them. This will take some leadership and wordsmithing. Again, it's important to have a notetaker who can synthesize the ideas.

The first draft will not be perfect, but the brainstorming will get the creative juices flowing.

3. Translate Your Values into Goals
Once you've identified your goals and you have an idea what each means insofar your family goes, translate these values into goals. The goals could be relational, social, cultural, faith-based, or financial. For example:

Value: Connection. (*Our family defined this as, "If you feel connected, you are not alone. We are connected to each other and to God and the larger world."*)

Goal: *Our goal is to have at least one holiday and one vacation all together as a family each year.*

Depending on life seasons, your family values may change over the years. As for the related goals, those tend to change more frequently. What should stay consistent, though, is your family mission statement.

Capturing a Common Purpose Through a Family Mission Statement

A family mission statement should be general enough to be a long-term directional guide, not a narrow accomplishment. At the same time, it needs to be succinct and capture your family's guiding principles and philosophy so clearly that everyone can easily understand it and might even commit it to memory.

Your mission statement is aspirational. It reaches for ideals that represent the core values you have determined. It also takes into consideration the stakeholders—everyone impacted by your family's purpose and mission.

A good family mission statement can be broken into an **overriding statement**, a **philosophy**, and a **directive.**

The **overriding statement** provides the tone of the family's mission. For example: Our mission is to be stewards of the blessings we have received, to recognize and support our family members and their individual needs, and to use the excess for the benefit of others.

The **philosophy** captures the family's highest priorities. For example: We believe a balance between education, mental health, and physical health is crucial to a happy life. Everyone in our family belongs, and we love them unconditionally. *We encourage each family member to use their strengths in a productive way for the greater good of society.*

The **directive** is a touchstone for future decisions. For example: Our financial resources are to be invested wisely and spent in support of our family's education, mental health, physical health, and charitable purposes.

Once the family mission statement is established, it must be communicated and re-communicated at the start of every family meeting.[3]

---

3   For additional resources to incorporating family values and developing your family mission statement, visit www.TheGreatestGiftBook.com.

Consider Having a Family Ideal

Several families that I interviewed felt that their transition was smooth because of their family values expressed as a memorable phrase, a slogan they recall as a touchstone—a family ideal. These can be as simple as these sayings:
- Never eat the seed corn.
- Live simply, love abundantly.
- Be kind every time.
- Be helpful, honest, and happy.
- Focus on the donut, not on the hole.
- Don't lose the forest for the trees.
- Do God's will.
- Love others as you would have them love you.

An ideal is different from a mission statement in that it's just one simple phrase, not a three-part statement.

Counselor's Insights

I wonder if Uncle George knew the importance of developing a common purpose when he created the family investment partnership. Did he know the foundational gift he was providing to Karen, Colleen, Kathleen, Mike, and Sean? I believe he knew instinctively the importance it would have to the family dynamics.

Regardless, establishing a common purpose fostered cooperation, trust, and a strong connection that enabled a smooth transition of company ownership.

As Sean mentioned, these endeavors to find a common purpose come with challenges. Wherever there is connection, conflict is sure to follow! They go hand in hand.

Conflict is inevitable in *all* relationships, including within families. In fact, conflict within families is more the rule than an exception. The goal is to move through conflict in such a way as to maintain connection.

To do so, we must avoid what renowned psychologists Drs. Julie and John Gottman call the four horsemen of criticism, contempt, defensiveness, and stonewalling.[4] When any of these "horsemen" show up in conflict, it leads to hurtful communication and, eventually, destroys connection.

The four horsemen research and tools are foundational for healthy communication, which is pivotal for the successful development and maintenance of family purpose. And while I only touch on the first horseman here, all of them are important.[5]

Horseman One: Criticism

When we are in conflict, emotions run high, and we naturally focus on what the other party is doing or saying that bothers us or we disagree with. It usually involves a *you*-led statement, and it typically includes an absolute qualifier.

Examples of you-led statements are:
- "You always talk over me."
- "You never let me finish."
- "Of course, you get the final say on things."

Criticism hurts the individual and our ability to connect. In fact, criticism leads to a *dis*connect, a break in effective communication.

---

[4] The Gottmans specialize in marital stability. Read more about their theory in this Gottman Institute blog post: bit.ly/FourHorsemenTheory.

[5] For more information on the four horsemen theory, visit www.gottman.com or www.TheGreatestGiftBook.com.

When you feel in conflict, rather than lash out with you-led statements, make a U-turn. Start from the inside—that is, identify how you feel and what you need, then mindfully state grievances with an "I feel . . ." and an "I need . . ." statement. One without the other is incomplete.

When you state how you feel without stating what you need, it can leave the other person feeling helpless, unsure what to do about how you feel. This, in turn, can lead to conflict or misunderstanding for either you or the other party.

The same goes for stating what you need without also explaining how you feel. On its own, an "I need . . ." statement lacks perspective and empathy for the other party.

But when you pair how you feel with what you need, it allows the listener greater capacity to understand your needs.

Together, an "I feel . . ." and "I need . . ." statement foster the safest environment for communicating.

The simple rule of starting with *I* rather than *you* makes all the difference in avoiding criticism. It helps you take responsibility for what you can, which builds an environment of safety and appreciation. It also helps you to stay regulated so that you can remain in the conflict rather than shut down.

Examples of I-led statements are:
- "I feel overlooked."
- "I'm upset. I feel unimportant in this discussion."
- "I feel like I have no say."
- "I'm angry. I feel my work is being discarded."

Clearly identifying what you feel is an important and hard step. If you can do this first, your chances of communicating effectively increase significantly.

But don't overlook the empowering second part of the formula, stating what you need to best support you in what you're feeling. This could be something you need from yourself or from others.

Sometimes even just expressing the feeling is the need. This could sound like:
- "I feel ignored. I just needed to say that."
- Or sometimes it is straightforward and logistical:
- "I feel ignored. I need to know we will vote on this before a decision is finalized."

The "I feel . . ." and "I need . . ." structure to communicating is simple yet effective.

⁂

The horseman of criticism can show up even in the simplest disagreements over what your family values and goals are. Or it can be rooted in disagreements over direction.

Take, for example, an imagined interaction between Sean and the other members of the family investment partnership. Imagine one of them criticizing another by saying, "You're putting too much emphasis on this company's social impact."

Now, consider how differently the same message would come across if they were to say, "I feel like this company is being dismissed too easily. I need to know we will research specifically how this company treats its employees."

Rephrasing the same idea as an "I feel . . ." and "I need . . ." statement would allow it to be received quite differently.

In my work with clients—especially couples and families—I have witnessed how using "I feel . . ." and "I need . . ." statements transform the nature of a conflict.

Tangible Tools for Managing Conflict

- **Avoid criticism.** Shy away from you-led statements that usually carry absolutes and judgment. Avoiding criticism helps maintain healthy communication.
- **When there is conflict, identify how you are feeling.** Are you overwhelmed, angry, confused, or disappointed? If so, say what you are feeling.
- **Next, identify what you need.** Do you need more time, information, or assurances, or maybe a five-minute break?
- **Stay regulated.** As best you can, try to remain calm and connected to those with whom you are in conflict.

⁣⁣⁣⁣⁣⁣⁣⁣⁣⁣⁣⁣⁣

In Short | Foster engagement among your heirs. This will help them feel connected so they can overcome any temptation to feel jealous when they have to share an inheritance with others.

Another way to unite and orient family members around a common purpose is to make sure everyone knows their family story, which is what we'll turn to in the next chapter.

2

Share Your Story

*Happiness does not consist in having what you want
but in wanting what you have.*
~Confucius

At least twice a year, my colleagues and I organize a fly-fishing trip. We invite clients who already enjoy the sport as well as some who want to learn. It's a great way to socialize and enjoy the outdoors.

This is one of the traditions passed down by Uncle George and his business partner, the late Lou Paul. They loved fishing, and over the years they taught me and countless others how to fly-fish.

Every spring, we head northwest to Harpster Farm—or Evergreen Farms, as it's officially known—in the Spruce Creek Valley, fishing the same

Principle 2:
Share Your Story
Destructive Emotion:
Shame
Constructive Emotion:
Appreciation
Proposition:
Perspective grounds you.

waters President Jimmy Carter and First Lady Rosalynn Carter regularly fished.

Located on one of the largest dairy farms in Pennsylvania, Harpster Farm is famous for raising trophy trout.

The grass alongside the stream is always freshly mowed, providing easy access to the water. The willow trees anchoring the stream banks are so old, their branches sweep the surface of the stream and provide restful shade when the sun is at its peak.

The farm is just two-and-a-half hours from our office, but it feels like another world all together. It is a fisherman's paradise.

In 2012, like we always do, my partners and I sent out invites at the end of February for the trip in late April. We had a list of six guests who were excited to join—one beginner and five repeat fishermen.

A week before our scheduled trip, the weather forecast reflected an unseasonably cold spell with below-zero temperatures at night and a high of 45 degrees during the day at Spruce Creek. Oh boy!

One by one, everyone canceled except my guest, Charlie . . . the beginner.

Charlie knows everyone. In the seven years I had known him by then, every time we'd meet for lunch, we'd get interrupted at least twice by someone coming over to say hi to him. Charlie is easy to be around, and everyone he meets is his friend, so much so that I nicknamed him "The Mayor."

Charlie was so excited to learn fly-fishing that he was willing to take a chance on the weather. Plus, he didn't have a lot of flexibility in his schedule, so he knew if he didn't go fishing with me that day in April, he likely wouldn't have a chance to go anytime soon.

In anticipation of our trip, his family surprised him. For his 60th birthday, they got him everything he'd need to go fly-fishing—the best rod and reel, vest, waders, boots, and a whole box full of artificial flies.

He really wanted to try everything out. So, we went.

I picked up Charlie after breakfast, and we drove the three hours to the farm, talking about this, that, and the other, everything from hobbies to taste in music.

We rolled up to the cabin a little after 1:00 p.m. and assembled our gear. The good news was that we had three quarters of a mile of stream entirely to ourselves. The bad news was the weather—42 degrees and overcast. Not ideal for fishing.

Charlie's setup was top-notch, the most state-of-the-art gear available. But even the best gear can't prevent a tangle.

I spent most of the afternoon freeing Charlie's line from a bush or a tree, adding new string leader, and tying on new flies, all while giving polite pointers on his casting technique. I was his de facto fishing guide, happy to help, and really hoping he would catch something.

By 4:30 p.m., it started snowing. Picture the two of us, knee-deep in the creek, while big, fat snowflakes were falling from the sky.

Then it happened.

Charlie saw his strike indicator bounce and felt a tug on his line. He lifted the tip of his rod, set the hook, and carefully brought in an eight-inch brook trout. He did it! He caught his own fish—the first of many caught (and released) over the ensuing years. I couldn't be happier for him!

Once the cold became too much to bear, we washed up and drove the half-mile to the Spruce Creek Tavern to warm up. Over a cold beer and a burger—and with a big grin on Charlie's face—we reminisced about the day.

After dinner, we headed to the cabin and built a fire. That's when Charlie told me his story.

When Charlie was just 14, his dad left their family. The oldest of five kids, Charlie started working odd jobs to help supplement the household income. His mom did everything she could to keep the household together, but still, everything was a struggle. Food was scarce, new clothes were out of the question, let alone a trip out of Philadelphia!

No one in his family had ever gone to college, but this was no deterrent to Charlie. He was determined to get a degree that would help him get a good job, become self-sufficient, and support his mother and younger siblings. So, Charlie got into Temple University in Philadelphia where he could commute from home. This was cheaper than living on campus, plus it allowed him to keep working.

The day after Charlie graduated, he started his job at a corporate real estate brokerage firm. He worked extra hours and constantly asked for new projects. His work ethic and determination were noticed at the highest levels of the firm, which lead to him becoming the youngest broker to ever be given a territory.

Despite having been in the industry for almost forty years, and despite he and his wife having amassed a personal balance sheet of over $10 million, Charlie shared with me that he still had severe anxiety when it came to money—especially running out of money. In fact, he had trouble sleeping when thinking about retirement. He believed he could neither slow down nor retire.

I could feel Charlie's pain and anxiety.

"Do your kids know your story?" I asked.

"Of course they do."

"But do they know what motivates you to work so hard? Do they know the sacrifices you have been making since your early teens?"

He broke down sobbing.

Jill tells me this type of emotional reaction is when she knows her clients have become most vulnerable, when they have made good progress in their introspection and in their therapy. I am not a therapist, but uncomfortable as I may have been, I was able to find the words to encourage Charlie to share his story.

It's not easy for me to admit, but I have similar anxiety about money. By no means am I comparing my upbringing to Charlie's, but as one of six children, I became fixated as a child about being able to buy whatever I wanted, whenever I wanted. My college friends were the first to point this blind spot out to me. While they called me cheap, I'd rebuke them by saying I was thrifty.

This brought to mind the joke Charlie and I often repeated as we compared our children's high-school experience and family vacations over the years.

"If there's a 'next life,'" one of us would say, "I want to come back as my kids!"

I have also heard others say, "Our kids have no idea how good they have it."

Our children's financial situations were much different than ours were growing up. This is what makes it so important for them to hear our story, our perspective.

Telling your story doesn't have to be negative. The purpose is simply to provide perspective. Your story shaped your personality and explains—for better or worse—your priorities and point of view. So, share stories often.

Being vulnerable about ourselves through honest storytelling reinforces trust and models open communication. Confiding in our children lets them know we trust them with the most personal details of our lives. Sharing all kinds of stories—successes and failures, achievements and difficulties—allows them to relate to our worldview.

Many cultures celebrate the oldest members of their family as elders. In this context, elders are defined as educators, thought leaders, and philosophers, not just people who are old. And elders are usually regulated and measured. They're in the best position to listen openly and dispense some of the wisdom they've collected over a lifetime of experience.

An elder is more apt to say, "It's been my observation . . ." than "Well, let me tell you . . ." The difference is an observance of a particular situation versus advice on what to do or how to live. As you age and consider the legacy you would like to leave, think of your role as an elder, sage, and storyteller.

Wisdom is best shared through storytelling. Storytelling creates perspective.

The Value of Sharing Your Origin Story

Recently, my client Sam shared with me a video he had recorded for his children. It was a simple video, shot on his smartphone. In it, he talked about his childhood, including some of his struggles and what life was like for him growing up.

Sam planned to share the video with his family to remind them of their roots, to emphasize their core values, to share lessons he had learned along the way, and to impart wisdom.

Watching this video made me realize, once again, that *we all have a story*. But this was the first time I heard of someone using their smartphone to record and share their story.

Making sure your family knows your roots also helps instill perspective—what we can also refer to as a *positive state of heart*.

Consider what your children's reaction might be to inheriting wealth—be it $10,000 or $100 million.

They might shrug their shoulders, thinking, I deserve this . . . After all, I was born into this family!

Or, if there's disappointment at the lack of zeros at the end of their inheritance, they might they be resentful.

It could be that they might be mortified receiving a sizable inheritance, feeling uncomfortable. Ashamed, even.

Or they might have a slightly different attitude, thinking, How blessed I am to receive this wealth . . . I will work hard to be a steward of this inheritance.

Beneficiaries' attitudes, emotions, and behaviors will be guided by their state of heart, their perspective—whether they feel entitled, harbor a grudge, are enveloped in shame, or respond with appreciation, with grace.

Grace. It's not the first word that comes to mind when thinking of an inheritance, but it certainly is a positive emotion to be instilled and reinforced, not only in your life but also in the lives of those who look to you as their parent or grandparent.

Across religions, grace is defined as the spontaneous, unmerited gift of divine favor—blessings that cannot be earned and given without asking for anything in return.

Giving without looking for something in return is the human manifestation or display of grace, and charitable giving is one way of reinforcing such grace. Demonstrating grace through charitable acts during your lifetime creates practice so beneficiaries can experience that grace when assets are distributed through an inheritance. (We'll talk more about giving in the seventh principle.)

But not everyone sees an inheritance as a gift of grace. For many it comes with a feeling of guilt or shame. Both are destructive emotions. Inheritors may not value the assets they receive the way their parents and grandparents did. They may not fully understand the story of how your family acquired their wealth.

This stresses the importance of telling your family story and helping your family know their roots, creating perspective and exemplifying a positive state of heart.

Some folks choose to write a book about their family story and self-publish it to share with their kids, grandkids, and those that may someday follow. Others get their stories published for the world to read, with the biographies of entrepreneurs often telling of humble beginnings, hard work and sacrifice, and the success that eventually resulted.

In some cases, these stories are incredibly personal, including tragedies that plagued the family, birth stories, and love stories. In other cases—like with what Sam did—it's a simple video to capture an origin story. Today, there are many websites and apps available to help you tell your story. Consider investing in one to help you on your way.

However you do it, capturing your story will help your descendants know their story, their roots. You have a story, so tell it. And tell it often. Also share what you're most proud of.

When our kids were little, Jill and I took a parenting class from our friend Lisa Corcoran. She often used a phrase that stuck with us: "Water what you want to grow."

As you share what you're most proud of, you're "watering" the source of pride, that which you want to grow. Water it by talking about it, weaving it into your stories. If you are proud of your hard work, tell stories about what it was like in the early days building your business. If you're proud of obstacles you've overcome, share those.

If you're like most of us, there may also be things you're *not* that proud of—the way you responded in adversity, perhaps. But if you're thankful for what you learned from the event, share that.

It's important that your children and grandchildren know that you have failed. They'll learn more from you sharing your failures than only sharing your victories.

The Danger of *Not* Telling Your Story

On November 27, 2020, the *New York Times* printed an article about Resource Generation, an organization that campaigns against the merits of capitalism.[6] This group includes a network of inheritors estimated to control assets of more than $20 billion.

The article, called "The Rich Kids Who Want to Tear Down Capitalism," features four individuals who have hired expensive lawyers to find ways to terminate their trusts and dismantle the estate plans laid out by their parents and grandparents.

Rather than reinvesting and growing their inheritance, these beneficiaries are looking for ways to accelerate trust income and principal payments so they can redistribute wealth to underserved populations and support more equitable economic infrastructures.

Embedded in Resource Generation's philosophy is the assumption that all wealth comes from oppressive behavior by businesses and their owners. As such, these benefactors view themselves as disruptors who are seeking to reverse the "stolen land, stolen labor, and stolen lives" that created their inheritance.

But from my experience, some of the most generous people I know are founders of businesses who have always treated their employees as part of their family.

I cannot help but wonder how many of their members are aware of the origin stories of their parents and grandparents, if they know the full story of how the family wealth was built over

---

6   Zoë Beery. "The Rich Kids Who Want to Tear Down Capitalism." *New York Times*, November 27, 2020.

time and the struggles and sacrifices that were required along the way. Instead, these "rich kids" are disgusted and feel guilt and shame over their inheritance—far from the feelings of appreciation and grace described earlier.

This emphasizes the importance of living a positive example of gratitude, sharing origin stories, and practicing a balance of charity and stewardship as methods to combat guilt and shame.

In his book *Life Is What You Make It*, Warren Buffett's youngest son, Peter, describes this feeling as "gift guilt."[7] Buffett suggests that privileged people know their good luck is undeserved. They want to enjoy the things that come their way, yet their conscience makes this difficult. This leads to resentment, which, in turn, leads to shame for feeling resentful.

If you can relate, how can you savor your good fortune? Start by acknowledging gift guilt. Next, tell your story. This will help ease some of the negative feelings that may come from receiving a large inheritance.

The Challenge of a Joint Vacation Home

"I want you to sell the beach house when I am gone," Grandmom told me during our estate-planning meeting.

Sell the home? Why would she want to sell it?

Grandmom and Grandpop had owned their beach house since the 1980s, and it's where their four children, 11 grandchildren, and 15 great-grandchildren formed some of our fondest memories.

This was an extraordinary beach house, not because of its size or grandeur, but because it was an annual meeting spot for our extended family. Despite only having four bedrooms, anyone who

---

[7] Peter Buffett. 2010. *Life Is What You Make It: Find Your Own Path to Fulfillment*. Crown Publishing Group.

wanted to visit was welcome anytime! Grandmom would always find a way to accommodate all of us.

The home was just a couple of blocks from the beach where we'd boogie board, fish, enjoy boardwalk rides and junk food, get sun-burned, and head home to gather around the table—our feet still sandy from the beach—for what Grandmom called "early-bird dinners."

Grandpop predeceased Grandmom by almost 10 years, but the beach was still my grandmother's happy place. It remained so all the way to the end of her life.

To plan for the day when she would no longer be with us, Grandmom, my dad, and my aunts asked me if I'd assist with her estate planning, something I considered a great honor.

So, when my grandmother said she wanted me to sell the house after her passing, I wanted to object. I knew better, though. Instead, careful not to sound disrespectful, I asked, "Grandmom, why would you want to sell the beach house?"

She gave me her usual warm, calming smile, then told me the story behind her wish.

Turns out there had been a family vacation home in Grandmom's family. That home had been passed from one generation to the next. But rather than be a blessing, it caused immense turmoil. Among my grandmother's cousins, especially, there were drawn-out conflicts around the management and upkeep of the home.

"I wouldn't ever want to see a home drive a wedge between all of you . . ." she told me. "That's why I want to sell the home and split the proceeds among my four children. And if any of them want to carry on the family tradition of having beach vacations, well, they'll have to use some of the money and figure that out for themselves."

Grandmom was brilliant. In her view, selling the house was instrumental to keeping the family peace, and in doing so, her decision was an act of grace.

||||||||||||

Over the years, I've met or heard of countless families where a shared home led to a breakdown in relationships.

Issues among those who inherit a joint vacation property often include fair use—who gets to use the property, how often, and when—and, of course, financial challenges.

Siblings usually have conflicting desires insofar as when and how often they'd like to use a vacation property. Some may not be able to use the property at all due to their life and family circumstances or location of their primary home, yet they may still be expected to contribute to the upkeep.

As we all know, though, homes are expensive to maintain and manage, plus they require a lot of time. On top of that, someone must take care of the running of the home, paying the bills, even dealing with contractors and upkeep.

Without a well-thought-out plan that everyone can agree upon in dealing with these topics, conflict is inevitable. It can even cause a permanent break in the relationship.

There are ways in which families can share a vacation home. In *Saving the Family Cottage*, Stuart and Rose Hollander along with Ann O'Connell provide suggestions for how to plan for the successful transition and upkeep of vacation properties, including the various legal structures that can be used to fulfill the family wishes.[8]

---

8   Stuart J. Hollander, Rose Hollander & Ann O'Connell. 2017. *Saving the Family Cottage: A Guide to Succession Planning for Your Cottage, Cabin, Camp or Vacation Home*. Nolo.

As with many aspects of estate planning, the best outcomes I have observed with succession of vacation homes have come with clear communication, a common vision, and clearly defined roles and responsibilities—topics we'll discuss in the remainder of this book.

IIIIIIIIIIIII

When you know your roots, you'll know whether your family has "old money," that is, native wealth, or whether you have "new money," first-generation or immigrant wealth, being the first generation to have accumulated substantial financial resources.

If you're in the latter category, you may have started with little or no money and built a business or collection of assets through hard work, disciplined spending, self-sacrifice, and delayed gratification.

However, you are also navigating new financial territory—one your ancestors may not have had to navigate before. Most financial concepts may be completely new to you.

Managing an investment portfolio, hiring and firing advisers, and outsourcing investment management, legal, and accounting responsibilities are tasks your parents may not have had. As a result, it was never modeled for you.

Likewise, planning for a transfer of wealth is also new.

Native wealth, on the other hand, is when your family's wealth has been passed down one or more generations. If you fall in this category, you may have grown up with wealth, financial responsibilities, and regular conversations about money.

Wealth and the conversations that come with it is something that may have always been there, and you are comfortable with it. Your standard of living, perspective, spending habits, and expectations are reflective of your family's multiple generations of wealth, guidance, and institutional knowledge.

While wealth transfer may have been a topic of conversation at family meals, it doesn't mean it's always gone without flaws (as you'll see in some of the stories in this book). It may also be why you chose to read this book.

Sharing Your Story to Model a Healthy Perspective on Money

It's not always as simple as knowing you are someone with immigrant wealth or native wealth. If you have enough of an age gap between your children and you acquired your wealth sometime between the birth of the older children and the birth of the younger ones, the older and younger children will have an entirely different experience of and relationship with money.

That was the case for Sam and Judi Johnson and their four children. There was a gap of 15 years between their eldest two and the youngest two.

When the first two were little, Sam and Judi were still establishing their business. They had limited financial resources and lived with the typical sacrifices that come with establishing a business and a family. But in the next 15 years, the Johnsons amassed more than $50 million in net worth, and then they had two more kids.

While the two generations of children were raised by the same parents in the same household, they had *very* different financial situations. Sam described the difference as, "When we travel, the younger two are allowed to eat from the mini fridge at hotels—but don't tell the older two!"

His comment was tongue in cheek. Sam is happy his family can enjoy traveling without watching where every dollar is spent. And based on his children's experiences, it is safe to expect the younger ones will be less careful with their spending than the older two.

This highlights how habits and upbringing inform children's behavior. It could be said that *perspective is caught, not taught.* Children follow their parents' example when it comes to behavior and habits.

Whether you are a person of significant means, or whether you've simply worked hard enough that money no longer is a big issue for you and your family, you'll want to model the type of perspective on money that you'd like your children and grandchildren to exhibit someday.

A part of how you model a healthy perspective on finances is by sharing your family story. Include stories that involve your children and experiences you have had together. Don't forget to share what you are proud of and what you wish for your family to be proud of.

Empower your beneficiaries with the facts—the full story of how you or your ancestors created your family wealth. Without this information, peer pressure and others' perception could give root to shame and guilt.

On the other hand, sharing your origin story and setting a good example with your lifestyle provide the most solid defense against shame.

How to Share Your Story

I have three clients who have taken the time to publish their stories as autobiographies, sharing hard-earned lessons and life wisdom. Writing an autobiography or a memoir is a big undertaking. It takes lots of time and resources. Fortunately, there are online resources that can help you through the process. (Visit www.TheGreatestGiftBook.com where we offer some tools that can help you organize and publish your story.)

But not everyone has the luxury of time to document their story in book form. Fortunately, that's not the only way to share your story. Jill's cousin David Ingerman—a dedicated husband, father, brother, son, and entrepreneur with boundless energy and charisma—introduced us to the concept of digitally documenting his life.

After he was diagnosed with terminal cancer, David subscribed to a website that regularly sent him question prompts. He shared his entries with a select group of family and friends. The stories included memories and experiences along with updates on his medical battle. At times, the site prompted recipients to submit stories involving David.

David received a lot of responses to these stories, and the feedback was an incredible source of encouragement and love for him.

A few weeks before his death, David told Jill, "It is amazing. Every living person should feel the love I feel right now."

David died in 2023 at the young age of 60. Thankfully, his sons know his story and will continue to reflect on the lessons he was able to share—including those he documented during his two years of capturing his journey.

Counselor's Insights

Commitment to a family, tribe, or community has long been fostered through the art of storytelling and legacy sharing. History is replete with gifted storytellers who shaped world events with their ability to cultivate belonging and commitment, fostering an understanding of culture, and building a sense of identity. This includes authors of the Bible, historians through the ages, and elders in cultures around the world.

Matthew—the disciple who penned the first of the four Gospels in the Bible—outlines a long list of names that made up Jesus's lineage. I suspect Matthew included the list so his readers would understand the complicated path of Jesus's ancestry. This, in turn, would help them feel more part of the story, making Jesus more human, more one of us.

The description of all parts of Jesus's family lineage helps Christians feel like they belong. With belonging comes feelings of safety and compassion—both necessary and powerful components of group cohesiveness, health, and commitment.

Remember Charlie's story he told Sean at the fishing lodge? Over the years, to those who don't know the hardship Charlie faced, his commitment to his job and success may seem over the top. But once you hear his story, compassion and respect for his sacrifices take root.

Charlie also beautifully models resilience, an attribute all parents seek to instill in their children. Hearing about a parent navigating a tumultuous childhood might inspire children to aspire to the same: "If Dad could make it under those circumstances, so can I!"

For your children to see themselves in your story, though, they'll need to know *all* parts of them are welcome—their gifts as well as their struggles. So, be mindful when sharing your story to have a balance between pride and vulnerability. A compelling story needs both.

That's another reason I believe Matthew included Jesus's genealogy at the start of his Gospel. The list includes characters most of us wouldn't want to admit are related to us—a prostitute (Rahab), a polygamist (King Solomon), and a rapist and murderer (King David).

Jesus's family wasn't perfect. But then again, no one's is.

When you share your full story with your children, you inspire without the pressure of perfection.

Here's the best part: Telling your story—whether through journaling, using web-assisted tools, or using video—not only improves your memory, but it also reduces stress and depression.

Sharing your story improves your mood, and your mental health benefits in the process.

Tangible Tools for Sharing Your Story

- **Share your story with intentionality.** Reflect on what is important to you to share before doing so.
- **Share the good and the bad.** Share your triumphs and your failures. The goal is to instill pride in the family legacy, not burden your descendants with perfectionism.
- **Solicit feedback.** Ask family members how the story made them feel, what they related to, and what they didn't. Be curious about their reactions.

In Short | Help your children and grandchildren be grounded by regularly sharing your origin story and the story of their ancestors. Reinforce the sacrifices made to establish the family legacy. Appreciating the sacrifices you and those before you have made helps inheritors overcome feeling shameful about what they receive.

When your family knows your origin story, it may explain some of the traditions you hold dear. Successful families unite around family traditions, the next principle we will explore.

3
Forge Traditions

May you trust God that you are exactly where you are meant to be.
~Saint Teresa of Avila

We all have a need to belong and to know that we are enough. It's part of being human.

For parents, it's a challenge to instill this confidence in our children—that they, too, belong and are enough, that they are unique, that we treasure them because of *and* despite of their strengths, weaknesses, successes, and failures.

Most of us are comfortable doing this in the corporate world, though. We run profitable businesses by building strong teams where each person has a role to play. Each person belongs.

One of my favorite office activities each November is when we go off

Principle 3:
Forge Traditions
Destructive Emotion:
Loneliness
Constructive Emotion:
Belonging
Proposition:
Family culture is important.

site for a team-building event. One year, we went for a cooking class. But as financial-services people, we were all a little nervous about the creativity this class would require of us. The anxiety showed up as silence.

Our team was small at the time—there were just 10 of us, including two new members. We all fit comfortably around the instruction table. The usually chatty bunch didn't say a word when the instructor walked us through the recipes we were to make and enjoy for lunch.

I was on the dessert team of four, tasked with making an apple pie. Once we got our hands dirty and could laugh at our measurement mix-ups and cutting and trimming mistakes, the anxiety level dropped. With it, the noise level increased. At the same time, the smells of the various dishes started to permeate the air of the teaching kitchen.

By the end, we were all laughing and joking. The nervousness we had felt at the outset was gone. Everyone was comfortable, we all felt like we belonged, and the meal was delicious!

The picture we took after lunch has stuck with me. Everyone was grinning from ear to ear. Best of all, our two new team members were spontaneously situated right in the middle of the group.

|||||||||||||

The same team-building techniques you might be familiar with at the office can be applied at home, helping each family member feel like they belong. That they're part of a team.

Admittedly, this is not always easy. It is worth every ounce of energy, though. There is a direct correlation between relationship building, a strong family culture, and the successful transfer of wealth.

As parents and grandparents, we can make a bid for connection day in and day out, but our children and grandchildren need to reciprocate. That starts with them feeling like they belong, that they are enough. Without that, they won't have the courage or desire to connect.

If they feel left out, there's no foundation of trust. Instead, there's disenchantment, self-isolation, and loneliness, all of which lead to fear.

These feelings are toxic. Plus, they grow with time, becoming key elements of conflict after parents die.

One antidote to feeling left out is having family traditions that support the fact that everyone belongs. These can range from simple, everyday traditions revolving around the dinner table—like the way you share about the events of your day—to larger, seasonal events centering around holidays and family vacations.

Can't think of what your traditions are? Start one! It is never too late to put in the effort to forge a new tradition.

Bonding over Meals

Sharing a meal as a family is the perfect time to connect, debrief, and destress. Sadly, TV, smartphones, and too many activities have hijacked family meals. According to a OnePoll study from 2022, the average family ate together only three times a week.[9]

Some families do recognize the importance of mealtimes together. One such family is the Gilroys, friends of ours who place a high priority on an uninterrupted family meal tradition.

A few years ago, the Gilroy family decided to adjust the time of their family dinner to accommodate everyone's schedules. To

---

9   Simona Kitanovska. "Average American Only Spends 3 Dinners a Week with Loved Ones, Poll Shows." *Newsweek*, August 5, 2022.

them, the need to be together is more important than eating at a set time. Some nights, they only have dinner at 9:00 p.m. But so be it.

I also know of a successful, multi-generation family business where noon-time family lunch has become an honored tradition. Charlie, the patriarch, started this tradition over 20 years ago when his eldest son joined the business.

Nowadays, all four of his children are leaders within the company, and they still meet for lunch each day at noon—no exceptions. Employees, vendors, and customers all know and respect the sanctity of this tradition.

For many families, Sunday dinner is still a time-honored tradition, even after kids have left the home. Sunday dinner is always offered, there will always be a hot meal, and the door is always open for those who are able to make it.

The sacrifice required to host such a meal is significant; the work of meal planning, preparation, and cleanup not to be underestimated. But the reward—including the reinforcement of a sense of belonging—is immeasurable.

Need help and looking for more resources and ideas? Go to www.TheGreatestGiftBook.com for resources to help reinvent family mealtime.

Vacations for Connection

While shared meals create a sense of belonging, so does having shared adventures, common experiences, and family explorations.

Take the Corolini family, for example. Every five years, their extended family goes on vacation together. This includes their children and their spouses as well as all their grandchildren and their spouses (or soon-to-be spouses—engagement ring required).

Other than airfare, Jamie and Steph Corolini cover all expenses of the trip. They communicate the trip dates, arrival and departure cities, and itinerary well in advance so the others can block off time and book their tickets.

As for Frank and Julie Montrose, rather than going someplace different each time, the couple hosts family week at their beach house the first week of August every year. The predictability of dates and the fact that the senior Montroses cover most—if not all—of the expenses of the trip remove barriers to participating. It also nurtures a sense of belonging.

Their motto? "All are welcome, and all belong!" When there are more people than beds, the couple rents a neighboring house to comfortably accommodate everyone.

Holidays and Belonging

Holidays do not necessarily mean trips away. To my friend Rich Jacobs, Thanksgiving is and always has been his favorite holiday of all. Rich understands the need to share holidays, and he's accommodating if his kids aren't around at Christmas or Easter. But not so at Thanksgiving. Rich has claimed it as a non-negotiable family holiday.

The four-day extravaganza kicks off on Wednesday night with an open house to which Rich invites old friends, neighbors, and business associates. What started as a gathering of a small group of high-school friends and family now has dozens of people coming and going throughout the evening.

Thursday is reserved for the immediate family for a traditional Thanksgiving feast. As for the Friday and Saturday after Thanksgiving, those have become "family fun days" during which Rich and his wife plan age-appropriate activities for all to enjoy.

We've all experienced holidays becoming emotionally charged as families grow and kids get married, and not everyone opts for a solution like Rich's.

For most families, choosing which family adult children spend important holidays with can be tricky. And it gets even trickier once grandbabies arrive as every grandparent wants to watch their little ones open presents on Christmas morning!

No one can be everywhere at once, though, and it's rare that your children's spouses would willingly abandon their own family traditions. I don't blame them. When the time comes, I will want my children to maintain the traditions we have established, but I know that is an unrealistic expectation.

The McNulty family has found a workaround by hosting an annual Eve of Christmas Eve party so that as many people as possible can attend this early dinner and still have time to get to their Christmas destination. Offering flexibility to accommodate everyone is important to them.

But that's not all they do. The couple even *encourages* each of their children to spend Christmas day with their spouse's family. They have clearly communicated to their children why they created this tradition, explaining that it takes the pressure off trying to be everywhere at once. But even more importantly, it reinforces that they are included, that they belong—no matter what.

Visits for Engagement

Even without taking vacations as a family or having special traditions around the holidays, you can foster a sense of belonging by being intentional about connecting with your family. My parents and their "meet them where they are" mentality have been the best role models for doing this.

In her book *Aged Healthy, Wealthy & Wise*, author Coventry Edwards-Pitt outlines the keys to a vibrant later-life experience with the acronym AGED standing for agency, growth, engagement, and drive—all qualities that my parents exhibit.[10]

They have six children and 13 grandchildren spread out from Vermont to Philadelphia. Despite the distance, my folks go out of their way to connect with us all. They foster a tight bond with all their children and grandchildren.

Using Edwards-Pitt's words, my parents have high engagement.

I don't know where they get their energy, but Mom and Dad provide childcare services if any of us need a night or a weekend away. They also attend school events, sporting events, and any noteworthy event to which they are invited, often showing up with a tray of homemade cookies or chicken cutlets.

This drive to help and to stay connected has not only created a strong sense of belonging, but it may also be helping my parents to keep going. This, in turn, is keeping them healthier and happier than a life in solitude, thus adding to their longevity.

It has taken tremendous effort over many years, but my parents have used their agency to forge a close-knit, dedicated family that shows up for holidays.

Best of all, we all sincerely enjoy being with them.

A Creative Birthday Tradition

In *Reclaiming Home: A Family's Guide for Life, Love & Legacy*, Krista Gilbert beautifully describes a tradition started by her family many years ago.[11]

---

10 Coventry Edwards-Pitt. 2023. *Aged Healthy, Wealthy & Wise*. BP Books.
11 Krista Gilbert. 2016. *Reclaiming Home: A Family's Guide for Life, Love & Legacy*. Morgan James Publishing.

Imagine turning 13 and having your entire family show up! They don't just *show up*, though; they honor you with unique gifts and timeless advice. This is one of the ways the Gilbert family reinforces their value of unity.

When each child in the family turns 13, they are treated to a wilderness walk. Along the way, each older member of the family greets them and presents them with a personal gift, often homemade, that aligns with their strengths and interests. And with it, the family member offers some words of wisdom.

I cannot think of a more powerful message meeting someone where they are in life and reiterating a sense of belonging! The most important people in their lives shower them with love, inspiration, and the tools to take on their teen years.

||||||||||||

As we've all experienced, though, things don't always go this way, especially with family. Sometimes, things can go awry, leading to experiences of abandonment or a sense of *not* belonging.

What follows are two unfortunate events where this was the case. One demonstrates the importance of belonging through traditions. The other highlights the importance of making all family members—including non-blood relatives or in-laws—feel like they belong.

A Breakdown of Traditions

For more than two decades, I've had the honor of working with Mike and Sherry Smith. They've done amazing financial planning, used proactive and consistent gifting, and created trusts worth millions for their children, James and Tiffany, their grandchildren, and generations beyond.

The Smiths have also been diligent when it comes to tax planning. As you may know, the tax law in the United States allows for two types of tax-free gifts: annual exclusion gifts, and gifts against the lifetime exemption.

In 2023, the annual exclusion gift amount per beneficiary was $17,000. That means you could give up to $17,000 each to as many people as you want without them or you having to pay any tax on the gift.

Once you exceed this amount in a year, you enter the *lifetime exemption*, which was $12,920,000 in 2023. That means if you give someone more than the annual exclusion amount, the excess amount gets deducted from your lifetime exemption. Even as long ago as the 1990s, the Smiths embraced the benefits of these types of tax-free giving.

All seemed well until, as adults, James and Tiffany both settled several states away.

Mike and Sherry became resentful, and rather than taking time to visit their children and grandkids, they poured all their free time into their business, blaming their reluctance to visit their children on the geographic distance and their business obligations. At the same time, their kids' and grandkids' busy schedules became an excuse to skip visits back home.

Over time, the separation by miles grew into a relational chasm.

Mike and Sherry had beautiful homes in Colorado and the Dominican Republic—homes that stood empty most of the year. One year, the couple suggested a family vacation at one of those homes. The kids weren't interested. They didn't want to take a family trip anyplace else either.

The Smiths blamed the in-laws—their children's spouses—for not being supportive of creating a stronger family connection.

And when they got to see James, Tiffany, and their spouses, the couple made no effort to hide this opinion.

Considering the millions they had already stashed away for their children, Mike and Sherry transferred $60 million of their private company stock to a trust that neither included their son, their daughter, nor their spouses. Instead, this trust would provide for the health, education, and support of their grandchildren and generations to follow.

Decades later, the Smiths sold their family business for more than $100 million. Per their earlier trust arrangements, about $40 million would go to their original family trust for James and Tiffany—a huge success by any measure of estate planning.

Instead, Mike and Sherry were resentful. They didn't feel close to their children, and at one point, Sherry demanded that "I want the bulk of the trust assets to go to the grandchild who visits me the most." This was hard to hear, but that's how she felt.

After the sale, we had a meeting to update their estate summaries, current distributions to each beneficiary, and discuss changes to the tax law. I was surprised when Sherry asked me how they could *reduce* the size of the trusts they had created. *They wanted to give their entire estate to charity.*

Mike and Sherry felt they had given too much to their heirs who "didn't have the heart to visit or call, nor made any effort with their parents and grandparents."

Unfortunately, for trusts to avoid estate and gift tax, they must be irrevocable. For the first time in my career, I had to let someone know they *could not revoke* a gift to their descendants.

Since they couldn't change the trusts, Mike and Sherry changed their wills to bequeath their remaining assets to charity. In their case, giving everything to charity was neither a joyful nor a grateful decision; instead, it was the only option better than paying tax to the IRS at death.

Their charitable gift was a punishment for a perceived lack of effort on the part of their children and grandchildren.

Who is to blame for how things turned out for the Smith family? Mike and Sherry? Their children? The in-laws?

From my vantage point, Mike and Sherry have been—and continue to be—in denial regarding their part in how their family has grown apart. Not once have they expressed any self-awareness of their role in their family's disconnect, nor have they expressed any regret for their actions. And they've never acknowledged that the time they poured into building the business has caused irreparable harm to their family.

I know that Mike and Sherry aren't the only well-meaning parents who haven't the faintest idea that money can't buy love. Instead, it takes effort and sacrifice to be in a true relationship.

If you feel your relationships are strained, start working on rebuilding them *now*. Start by suggesting just one simple family tradition. Be the first to make the effort and continue trying to rebuild the relationship, with awareness that your first suggestion—and maybe even the second and third—may not be accepted.

When the In-laws Feel Like They Don't Belong

No matter how hard you work at fostering traditions, some family members may resist the efforts. For the Montgomerys, this was the case when their son Jackson married Lilly.

Try as they might, Lilly resisted embracing the Montgomery family culture. She didn't feel like she belonged, and years later, this became a major source of stress for everyone.

John's father and grandfather made their money in the cable TV industry, and since before John and Sue Montgomery were even married, the couple was endowed with trusts exceeding $50 million. An entrepreneur himself, John went on to more than *quadruple* their family's net worth.

Their lifestyle didn't flaunt their wealth, though. They certainly had vacation homes, took wonderful trips, and had nice things, but they were humble, fiscally conservative, and deeply grounded as a family.

The family's estate attorney, accountant, and I met annually with John and Sue, and they had used every estate-planning strategy they could to minimize taxes and accomplish their charitable and family goals. Their estates eventually paid very little estate tax, and the family was set for generations. Theirs was one of the best estate structures and plans I had ever observed!

At the time of their passing (Sue survived John by four years), the children each had a trust worth over $80 million after the payment of estate taxes.

I worked with each of the Montgomery children—Dana, Jackson, and Hunter—just as I had with their parents for the prior 10 years. Naturally, I also met their spouses. And in each case, I helped with their estate planning and life insurance needs.

There was no reason to doubt that I had built as trusting a relationship with them as I had with their parents.

But within a year of Sue's death, Jackson's wife, Lilly, started questioning all the Montgomerys' advisers. She demanded that several long-serving advisers be replaced. She launched forensic accounting to research unfounded suspicions and initiated dead-end projects that cost the family tens of thousands of dollars.

While these investigations turned up nothing, they caused irreparable damage within the family as the Montgomerys' other children were vehemently opposed to what their sister-in-law was doing. They pleaded numerous times with Jackson for Lilly to stop, but it seemed she had something to prove.

From the outside, it is difficult to understand how anyone who inherited $80 million could be unhappy. But as the adage goes, money can't buy happiness.

I attribute Jackson and Lilly's uneasiness and suspicion to feeling like they didn't belong.

Looking back, I recall John and Sue sharing stories of family vacations that, for some reason or another, didn't include Jackson and Lilly. John also shared that there wasn't a close bond between him and Lilly. Lilly was a successful audit partner at a notable firm, but John never invited her to be part of the family business, which undoubtedly caused jealousy and resentment over the years.

The chasm this created between the Montgomery children still exists to this day. Jackson and Lilly won't even speak with Dana, Hunter, and their families—something that has caused immense pain for the siblings.

||||||||||||

As we discussed at the outset of this chapter, family traditions create and reinforce belonging. By including everyone, no one feels left out. This can be as simple as regular family dinners, and as complex as an elaborate international vacation.

Be intentional about scheduling visits. Birthdays are a great excuse to celebrate each person and help them feel important. Reach out again and again, even if your children don't reciprocate at first.

Regardless of what traditions your family chooses, they should center around community and quality time, and underscore belonging.

A Letter to My Children

A year or so after her husband's passing, my client Sarah started a relationship with a kind and successful widower. Several of Sarah's children were vocal in their disapproval. They were adamant that the man was a gold digger.

When I traveled to meet with Sarah, she shared with me the pain she was going through. It seemed like her children's rejection of the relationship felt like they were rejecting her, that she no longer belonged.

This had a profound impact on me. On my flight back, I wrote a letter to my children. Since then, I've kept the letter in the lap drawer of my desk at home so they would find it if I died an untimely death. But by printing it in this book, my kids get to read it while I'm still around.

None of the insights will come as a surprise to them, though, as they're all young adults now, and I've been teaching them many of the ideas outlined in the letter.

Morbid as it may be, I read the letter from time to time. Though many years have passed since I first penned it, my feelings about these topics have not changed.

February 4, 2005

Zach, Ryan, and Kylie,

There are many values I want to instill in you directly during a long life together, but I'm writing this letter just in case . . .

Take care of Mom. She is the most amazing person in this world. Support her emotionally, financially, and when her knees give out, physically.

I have seen a lot of families fall apart when a widow starts a new romantic relationship or remarries. Mom is very smart. Support her decisions. And let me assure you, it's better for everyone that Mom finds a new soul mate once I pass. He'll never be as cool as me, but I don't believe that humans are made to live alone. It doesn't mean that Mom didn't love me, and it doesn't erase any of the memories we created together.

You three have a common bond that cannot be replaced. You are part of the same litter. No one else in this world has experienced the highs, lows, and in-betweens of our family and your common upbringing experience.

Never, never let money or "financial fairness" come between you and anyone you love, have loved, or will love. I have witnessed many situations where families quibble over belongings, and it breaks my heart they cannot see the personal property as a blessing.

Be grateful for what you have—no matter how much or how little. And remember, you can't take it with you when you're dead. From what I have observed, living by this mantra apparently is a lot harder than it sounds.

There are many of my qualities I hope you will have picked up over the years. I hope my "cheap gene" isn't one of those. I see it as a weakness that I often fight for every discount and emphasize frugality. I think you'll understand that these come from the fact that growing up, I didn't have enough money to buy brand-name clothes or discretionary items.

As a reminder, here's what your financial priorities should be.

1. Live within your means. If you earn $40,000 per year after taxes, spend less than $40,000 per year. To ensure you spend less than you make, budget. Plan your spending. Then work your budget. That means you must track your spending.
2. Save money. It's never too early to start saving. Your future self will be happy you did. Saving also creates good habits and discipline. You'll quickly recognize the difference between wanting something and needing something.
3. Invest wisely. Avoid risky investments. Take your time to study your options. Buy right. Look for value. Buy when others are afraid to, or when something is out of favor. Be a contrarian.
4. Use the 24-hour rule. When it comes to decision-making, Uncle Mike and I always use this rule. When you don't have a strong conviction about a big decision, let your subconscious help. Sleep on it. Sometimes, you'll figure it out overnight! And talk to people you trust, people who may have dealt with a similar question or decision.

It is my dream that you will always keep these perspectives that Mom and I have tried to instill in you: Have faith in God. Be connected. And love and support each other.

I love you and am incredibly proud of the person each of you has become. You are each amazing in your own way.

Love,
Dad

Counselor's Insights

Mike and Sherry Smith's story and their desire to revoke the trust they had established for their children, evoke feelings of helplessness and despair in the reader. The family was successful in so many ways. They used to have a deep love for their children and grandchildren.

So, what went wrong?

There are several psychological frameworks that offer a starting place to answer this question. Perhaps they had not attended to the grief of having "lost" their children to more distant homes and to families of their own.

Or maybe the family had mismatched love languages. For Mike and Sherry, love is expressed through gift giving, while for their children, it may be quality time.

It is also possible that the family lacked awareness of each person's individual needs, and they didn't communicate these needs either.

While this may all be true, I'll focus on two approaches that have been used by behavioral and social learning psychologists for decades: modeling and conditioning.

Mike and Sherry worked hard over the years to provide generous financial resources for their children that inevitably required a sacrifice of time and physical presence. They provided X (X being parental support in terms of resources over the years) and they were expecting Y to follow (Y being visits, phone calls, and a commitment to go on family vacations).

Both X and Y are valuable, but clearly are not equal expressions of value. Hold off on judging one as better or worse. Instead, simply acknowledge that they are different.

Can you model X while expecting Y in return?

When forging traditions, assess your X and Y—the behaviors you model and the conditioned behaviors you expect in return. Here's how:

- Consider what specific, conditioned behaviors you are hoping to see your children demonstrate as it relates to forging traditions or spending time together. The more specific the naming of desired behavior, the better.
- The Smiths, for example, were hoping their children would visit, call, or text regularly. Asking for an annual visit or a weekly call or text would have been a good start for them.
- Consider what behaviors you are modeling as they relate to these desired, conditioned behaviors. Ask whether your behavior demonstrates a willingness to put others' needs or preferences before your own (e.g., schedule, duration of gathering, or mode of communicating).
- Did the Smiths visit their children? Did they call or text as much or more than they expected in return?
- Did the Smiths visit when it was convenient for their kids' schedule instead of their own?
- Did Mike and Sherry chat with their kids and grandkids via text rather than expecting them to call, the senior couple's preferred mode of communication?
- Did the Smiths plan a family vacation that appealed to their kids' interests over their own?
- Assess whether your behavior shows a commitment to celebrating accomplishments or milestones that are important to those you are hoping to model.
- Did the Smiths attend birthdays, milestone events, graduations, or religious events that were important to their children even if they weren't necessarily important to them?

Elders in the family hold much power and influence over the tone and culture of the family system. Use that influence intentionally to create what you desire. How can you realistically expect what you don't give?

Doing so will likely feel self-sacrificial, front-loaded, and difficult at first. But it is a worthwhile investment in developing others, and they will reap benefits for years to come.

This reminds me of something my dear friend and author Krista Gilbert says: "Easy choice, hard life. Hard choice, easy life."

Make those hard choices *now*, whatever stage you are in, and you are setting yourself up for easier, more fulfilling experiences and relationships in the future.

Behavioral psychology also purports that *rewards work a lot better than punishment in shaping desired behavior*. Plus, they're a lot more fun to use!

Remember Pavlov and his salivating dogs? The reward of food proved much more effective in getting the dogs' salivation response than punishment would ever be.

Applying this in the context of creating traditions within families, requires that you understand what the rewards of spending time together would be for those in your family. This will vary by person and circumstance, and the best way to get to the answer is to simply ask.

Take-Away Tools for Forging Traditions

Here are some questions you can use to assess how you can use modeling and conditioning to forge traditions and create a sense of belonging. The first three questions are ones you can ask yourself. Those, along with the final three, are also questions you can ask your children and grandchildren.

1. Does the gathering provide access to age-appropriate activities?
2. Does the gathering allow for flexibility of schedule?
3. Have we made the gathering as easy as possible for all members to attend—both fiscally and physically?
4. What makes a family gathering or getaway appealing to you?
5. What makes it hard?
6. How can we make this easier for you to attend?

Of course, extrinsic rewards such as providing food and lodging help, but it is easy to forget about more nuanced rewards—like sending a clear message that everyone belongs, that they are important.

When both the extrinsic and intrinsic rewards are evident, it will motivate your kids to make getting together a priority. And it will set the stage for many good years of reciprocal relationships.

⸻

In Short | Family culture shows up through your traditions. Build on the traditions you already have. Grow them, encourage involvement, and find ways to make more of them. Feeling like they belong prevents inheritors from acting out, even if they feel lonely once their parents die.

Now that you have traditions unique to your family, it is important for everyone to further the sense of belonging by being clear about everyone's roles.

4
Define Roles

Perhaps the most important vision of all is to develop a sense of self, a sense of your own destiny, a sense of unique mission and role in life.
~Stephen Covey

From the outside, the Walsh family appeared to have it all—a horse farm in a picturesque part of eastern Virginia, four adult children, all with stable, productive lives, and 11 grandchildren. When I met them, though, Steve and Joanne Walsh were in a panic.

They were nearing their 80s, and despite having combined assets of more than $30 million, they had done *no* estate planning.

Joanne had inherited shares in a brick manufacturing business that had grown to be worth more than

Principle 4:
Define Roles
Destructive Emotion:
Contempt
Constructive Emotion:
Respect
Proposition:
Responsibility makes a difference.

$20 million, and Steve had built his advertising firm from scratch. Their horse farm was a hobby and barely broke even, but the value of the homestead, land, and barns had grown substantially during the time of their ownership.

With no planning, their eventual estate tax would be more than $5 million!

Our office assembled an advisory team—an estate attorney, the Walshes' tax preparer, and valuation experts. Within a year, the legal team had created six trusts and drew up new wills.

That year, Steve and Joanne Walsh made gifts of nearly $20 million to their children. These gifts included equity (shares of stock) in Joanne's family business and eight parcels of real estate.

In the process, the planning team saved the Walsh family more than half of the future estate tax. They were visibly relieved.

While this process was flawless, the same could not be said of the communication with their children.

Mark, their youngest child and only son, had the most entrepreneurial success, and he had amassed a sizable estate on his own. Previous versions of his parents' wills had named him as the executor of their estate. As a result, Mark expected this to remain unchanged.

Instead, Steve and Joanne named two of their three daughters as executor and trustee. Their logic was that Mark was so tied up with his businesses that he would not have the time needed for the proper administration of the estate and six trusts.

Normally, I place much emphasis on having family meetings (more about that in Chapter 9). In this family's case, though, we didn't call a meeting. Here's why.

From my perspective, Steve and Joanne seemed to have very open and frequent conversations with their children, including a long tradition of extended family dinners every Sunday with as many of their children and grandchildren as could join.

Plus, Steve had asked me for summaries of the progress made with their gifting. He and Joanne were planning on sharing those reports directly with each of their children over the Fourth of July weekend that year.

When they met with Mark and communicated their wishes, he was livid. Mark took the decision as a sign of disrespect. He was convinced that his parents didn't think him to be good enough for the job of executor. He may have also felt that his parents favored the sisters whom they appointed as fiduciaries.

For many months, Mark refused to speak to his parents—a first for their family.

Joanne confided in me that she wished they had been more deliberate in their delivery of the news. Instead, they had sprung the news on him before providing the logic behind their choice.

She and Steve were devastated by the fissure in the family relationship, and they went out of their way to reconcile with their son. They eventually had several very emotional one-on-one conversations with Mark. During those, they were able to reinforce their unconditional love and respect for their son. They were also able to help him see their rationale for choosing two of his sisters as executor and trustee.

Over time, these hard conversations brought healing. A year after the blow-up, Mark even admitted that he was relieved not to have to deal with the ongoing administration and tax compliance responsibilities of the family trusts.

The anxiety and suspicion Mark felt—along with the conflict they caused—were difficult for everyone to endure. But Steve and Joanne had the hardest task. De-escalating and resolving Mark's negative feelings could not have been settled by anyone but them.

I often wonder how different the relationships between the Walsh children would have been if Steve and Joanne did not communicate their choices during their lifetime. Mark's feelings of insecurity, of others being favored over him, and his bitterness would have been hard to reverse. His relationship with his sisters—especially the two asked to serve as trustees—would likely have been tarnished forever.

In hindsight, I regret not offering to help organize a family meeting to discuss the new structure. Such a meeting would have saved a lot of turmoil. Specific to establishing roles, it would have been better for everyone to hear about the strategy and decisions about roles and responsibilities directly from Steve and Joanne all at once.

Transparent communication during your lifetime is a blessing. Without it, there are too many unknowns.

Don't leave it to your heirs to read between the lines as to how you came to decide things, the fiduciaries you named, or how you value them as individuals.

The saying is true: information is power. Sharing information is a tremendous gift you can give during your lifetime. But if you're unable or unwilling to communicate what is important, your family can prepare for a bumpy ride when it comes to the transition of wealth someday.

Family Roles

No family is the same, and whether you acknowledge it or not, every person has a role in your family. The same is true when it comes to the roles everyone plays in the management of your family assets. Defining those roles is important and unique to each family. It is based on the human capital and skill sets of each member.

Roles in managing the family monetary assets are straightforward, but for anyone with a sizable inheritance, I strongly recommend that those roles be outsourced.

For roles that require a subject matter expert, I strongly advise that you hire professionals to be a resource. (More about that later in this chapter.) Doing so will maintain objectivity and remove conflicts of interest. This will also reduce—and hopefully remove—the possibility of conflict among family members.

Hired consultants must be held to the highest of each profession's industry standards in ethics and best practices, which is why I advise against having a family member in these roles. However, if a family member expresses interest in one of the professional roles, they could be required to join family meetings and engage with the hired professionals. (More about family meetings in Chapter 9.)

Finding a Suitable Role for Each Family Member

As seen in Mark's response to his parents' estate plans, even receiving a sizable inheritance devoid of love and respect is fraught with problems.

One way you can circumvent this challenge is to help each adult child find a role to play in the management of the family's financial *and non-financial* assets. Helping them find a role is better than assigning a role.

If roles don't emerge organically, carefully consider roles that match the skills and talents of each family member, then communicate your rationale for suggesting those roles.

As a parent, I know it's hard to objectively assess my children's strengths and weaknesses. I know them too well, and I have too much emotional attachment to them. Hence, using a consultant who can conduct a skills assessment along with a personality assessment may help your family pick the best role for each person.

Don't wait until after your passing to let family members step into these roles, though. The sooner they can try out a few roles, the sooner they will find how they can best participate in your family mission.

This sends a clear message of love and respect to your children and grandchildren. What's more, entrusting your heirs with responsibility and confidential information shows that you see them as being capable of receiving such information, that you respect them as an important part of the family.

Not only are they able to handle the information being shared; they are ready to play a role in the future of the family.

Jill has a favorite saying: "Our children become what is reflected in our eyes." If we believe they will be able to make good decisions, they will. If we act like we don't trust them or treat them as immature, they will lack confidence and act with indecision.

If roles have not yet been established in your family, start with the principles outlined in this book to determine where each family member can participate. Assess each person's talents, then challenge them to help promote a principle.

Here are some ways family members can engage in each of the principles. I also include a short description of what would be involved. Encourage even the youngest family members to participate and learn the different roles so they may take leadership positions in the future.

1. **Develop a Common Purpose** | *Coordinator of Events.*
   For estates not large enough to warrant establishing an

LLC or charitable fund, I had mentioned earlier that you could identify interests that everyone has in common, name a purpose to it, and have consistent and regular get-togethers that center around this purpose.

Managing Member of a Family LLC, or *Executive Director of a Charitable Fund.* This pertains to larger estates, and this person would be responsible for the management, communication, and collaboration with family—as guided by the mission of the entity.

2. **Share Your Story** | *Family Historian.* Interview ancestors to tell the story from the past, and document and communicate major family events and milestones as they unfold in the future. Consider publishing a book, a biography about a notable matriarch and patriarch who had a significant impact on your family or were the wealth creators.

3. **Forge Traditions** | *Fun Commissioner.* Make gatherings inclusive, fun, and easy to participate in, based on the family's shared interests and desired frequency.

4. **Define Roles** | *Chief Family Resource Officer.* Assess talent and interests. Identify strengths from an early age and provide the educational and mentorship opportunities to encourage those talents.

5. **Promote Humility** | *Spiritual Director* or *Gratefulness Coach.* Find opportunities to discuss and encourage curiosity about a higher power and spread regular messages of awe and gratitude.

6. **Nurture Independence** | *Parent.* This isn't an appointed role; it comes with the territory. Enforce natural consequences, accountability, discipline, and empowerment. Encourage failure as a means of personal growth.

7. **Encourage Giving** | *Strategist*. Understand the family's changing interests and desire to assist or incite change to develop an inclusive and ongoing gifting strategy.
8. **Create a Safe Environment** | *Non-parent Elder*. Provide coaching and guidance to younger family members and encourage growth in all aspects of life—not just money management.
9. **Overcommunicate** | *Family Meeting Coordinator*. Solicit family meeting topics and schedules, and help plan annual family meetings. Also collect feedback on meetings.

Think twice before considering outsourcing any of these roles. The effort each one requires is reinforcing the family member's role—they are included, and they are important. Their contribution to the family is vital and meaningful.

Developing Roles by Working Together

It is far better to talk about which role fits which family member best than to simply *tell* them what their role is within the family. Communication is about involvement—not directing or preaching or dictating mandates.

Working together to discern and develop the best role isn't something that comes naturally for many of us, though. It takes time, practice, and experience.

Take the Mallon family, for example. John and Mary Mallon established a family LLC for wealth transfer purposes. The LLC was to hold their lake home, an assortment of equipment leased to the family's trucking business, and John and Mary's investment portfolio. (Structuring the equipment to be purchased by the family LLC and then leasing it to the trucking company is a common way to shift trucking company profits to the LLC over time.)

What the couple didn't expect was for the LLC to have a crucial secondary effect of establishing family roles. John and Mary were able to witness the development of interests and talents of each of their three children.

Anne, a psychologist, took responsibility for managing the family's vacation home.

Luke, husband to their daughter Kate, had been running the family business and took on the responsibility of managing the leased assets.

Their youngest, Michael, coordinated the family business meetings. A schoolteacher by profession, he also enjoyed preparing reports and working with the accountants on tax filing, but this took an inordinate amount of time.

During a recent family meeting, Michael made the case for himself to start taking a salary as compensation for the extra effort. Until then, no one in the LLC had been paid a salary, but the sisters agreed that Michael should be compensated for his work. John and Mary couldn't be happier watching their children work through the conversation and come to this agreement.

From my experience, navigating family conversations such as this one—even if it includes healthy debate—is better to be done while parents are still alive and, if possible, in the room, as the children are often more motivated to keep the peace than if their mom and dad were no longer around.

Discerning parents would know not to step in to solve the issues or to referee the conversations, especially around establishing clear roles. Instead, they would invite directness and transparency.

Picking a Professional Team

The larger and more sophisticated a financial estate becomes, the more important it is to find advisers who understand the relevant decisions and tools to assist your family. Your advisory team, at minimum, must have an estate-planning attorney, a tax accountant, an investment consultant, and a life insurance professional. Each of these are specialists.

The advisory team may also grow to include specialists in bill-paying and bookkeeping, family relationship counselors, business succession consultants, and property management professionals.

Speaking of hiring a relationship counselor, when I once suggested to an entrepreneur that we discuss core family values at his next family meeting, he vehemently objected, saying, "I am *not* having a shrink at the family meeting!"

When I propose hiring a professional to help facilitate discussions around non-monetary topics, such a reaction no longer surprises me. To overcome the initial objection, I share examples of other families who have had great success employing outside resources as part of their advisory team.

Families with a large estate will need a professional support team with a diversified set of skills. While some support can come from within your family, legal, tax, insurance, and investment services should be left to paid professionals.

Legal Professionals

Hiring a generalist lawyer is a major mistake. Most law schools require only *one* estate and trust course to graduate. Instead, your attorney needs to be a trusts and estates (T&E) specialist with a graduate degree (an LLM) in taxation.

An LLM in tax law includes classes in estate planning, international taxation, and state and local taxation. Your attorney must be familiar with the tax nuances in your home state as well as the state where you retire, if that is not your regular home state.

In my home state of Pennsylvania, many clients move to Florida for retirement and become permanent residents there. Hence, it is common for T&E lawyers in Pennsylvania to also have expertise in Florida so they can maintain relationships with clients who relocate there.

It goes without saying that your lawyer must be admitted to the bar in your state, allowing them to practice law in that jurisdiction.

Accountants

Choosing a certified public accountant (CPA) also needs to be done with intention. While it may be tempting to stay with a long-term accountant rather than make a change, it is imperative that you switch when you've outgrown your accountant's level of sophistication. This is true even if, like was the case of one of my clients, your accountant is a friend and has helped you from the beginning when you were just starting out.

Similar to T&E lawyers, your CPA needs experience with complex tax solutions and deep knowledge of the federal, state, and sometimes international tax laws and regulations. Also, look for a CPA who is part of a firm that has subject matter experts that they can rely on when a unique question or problem arises.

Insurance Professionals

Life insurance and property insurance needs are dynamic. Specialists in each area are critical to being sure the coverages you buy are appropriate for the changing needs of your family.

One of the most common tax-planning mistakes is owning life insurance in the name of the matriarch or patriarch of a family. The death benefit would be included in their estate, which would trigger federal estate tax and, where applicable, state inheritance tax.

Sophisticated life insurance advisers will review the tax implications and performance of your policy portfolio. They will understand the importance of tax structures and know how market forces will impact the long-term performance of the policies.

As for property insurance, it is critical for protecting assets. With the increased frequency of weather events, having properly structured policies has become even more important.

One of our clients thought their vacation home in Florida was properly insured, but when a hurricane hit the area, their insurance company denied a water damage claim, asserting the water intrusion came from wind-blown rain, and they did not have wind coverage.

Protecting homes, vehicles, and recreational assets is important. Coverage to help safeguard against cyberattacks, identity theft, and travel risks—including kidnap and ransom—should be part of the conversation each year.

Investment Advisers

Investment advisers have a variety of service models. Find one which matches your needs. If you're an experienced investor that knows a lot about the markets, your needs are different from someone who doesn't have a lot of investment experience and needs education and handholding along the way.

Is the mentoring of your younger family members important to you? If so, make sure the investment professional is part of a firm with younger advisers your family can relate to. One of my clients wanted to make sure their daughter had a female role model to help educate and guide her. Likewise, if that's important to you, choose a firm with women on their investment team.

Of course, fees and structures are also important. Do not be afraid to ask for, challenge, and negotiate the proposed management fees. And be sure to get multiple proposals so you can analyze the different service models and fee structures between firms.

///////////////

Assembling the right team takes work, but having the right players around your advisory table is invaluable. So, be intentional about the professionals invited to serve your family needs.

In addition to having the proper credentials and experience in each area of expertise and having time to devote to you, an adviser must be . . .

1. **Attentive.** I have observed several situations where the name or reputation of one adviser drew a family to use them; however, they were not the best fit for the family and the rest of the team as they were too busy and inaccessible. An adviser needs to have space in their schedule to give your family the attention you require, especially at the onset of the relationship.
2. **Collaborative.** Avoid hiring power-hungry advisers who care more about being in control than working as a team. As such, the adviser should not seem like someone who has to be seen as the smartest person in the room.
3. **Holistic.** They should be willing and able to understand your goals and objectives—or help you arrive at them—before making a recommendation. They need to understand the big picture and the interconnectivity of each of the parts of your estate plan.

4. **Patient.** Planning takes time and things often change. You'll want to pick someone who won't rush the process or get impatient when changes are made.

The Role of a Fiduciary

When it comes to the roles of an executor and trustee, those are rarely filled by family members. But like with the Mallons, family members *can* fill these roles. Keep in mind, though, that these roles are legally defined and carry great power. As such, naming a fiduciary is a big decision for families.

A fiduciary is someone who manages money or property for someone else. The common fiduciary roles in estate planning are that of executor, guardian, and trustee.

Fiduciaries are held to a legal standard of care. For example, an executor is required to carry out the wishes of a decedent as expressed in their last will and testament. And a trustee is legally bound to follow the terms outlined in a trust. If either the executor or trustee fails to do so, they will be replaced and, in the extreme, could be sued for criminal damages.

Trustees are long-term fiduciaries once an estate has been settled and trusts are in place. Therefore, our discussion below will focus on the role of trustee. Trustees do not have to be trained in law or accounting. They must, however, uphold the following five duties:

1. **Duty of Care** | Prior to making a decision regarding the trust, a trustee must have a thorough understanding of the trust and make themselves aware of all material information and facts. For example, before making a principal payout, a trustee must understand the ages of distribution outlined in the trust.

2. **Duty of Loyalty |** Trustees must act without personal economic conflict. They must avoid taking excessive fees or bonuses from the trust. Trustee fees are necessary, but a periodic review of market trustee fees helps keep those fees reasonable.
3. **Duty of Good Faith |** Trustees must advance the interests of the trust and fulfill their duties without violating the law. Trustees can become personally liable for unlawful acts, even if acting in their capacity as trustee. This includes being compliant in tax matters.
4. **Duty of Confidentiality |** Trust provisions and activities are private and not intended to be disclosed publicly. Trustees must keep information about the trust confidential, including the terms, provisions, and values of the trust.
5. **Duty of Prudence |** A trustee must administer a trust with the degree of care, skill, and caution that a prudent person would exercise, such as hiring professionals to help with investment management and tax compliance. Hiring and managing professionals with expertise help trustees fulfill this duty of prudence.

The Beech Family and Their Dream Team

When it comes to assembling and working well with an advisory dream team, the Beech family knows a thing or two. James Beech was an executive his entire life and had amassed a fortune from the various companies he helped grow during his career. His résumé included some of the most recognizable and iconic consumer brands of the last 30 years.

James ran the Beech family meetings the way he ran a board meeting. He sent out an agenda several months in advance, though from year to year, there wasn't much difference in what was slated to be discussed.

Something else that didn't change was the timing of the annual family meeting—the second Tuesday in August. Even his advisory team (of which I was a part as the life insurance consultant) scheduled their family vacations around that date so we could attend. The team also included an estate-planning attorney, an accountant, and an investment adviser.

The predictable cadence of the meetings and the consistency of attendance provided multiple benefits, including that the family and the advisory team were all prepared and ready to collaborate and make informed decisions.

It was a model of efficiency.

There were no excuses to come to a Beech meeting unprepared. Because the agenda was consistent and published well in advance, we as members of the advisory team had ample time to do the work necessary to complete follow-up items, prepare reports and executive summaries, and brainstorm new ideas.

Some of the decisions that had to be made included items pertaining to a change in the family. If one of the children was getting married, for example, we would discuss if a prenuptial agreement was needed. If one of their children had a baby, we'd know it was time to fund a new 529 education savings plan. Or if there were changes in tax regulations, we'd work on adapting the legal structures of the estate.

The advisory team sent out information in advance to help family members prepare an opinion and debate the merits of each angle of a choice.

One year, there was a tax law change that we as the advisory team knew would be important to add to the agenda. Rather than wait to bring the topic up at the meeting, we had several conference calls to come to consensus on a recommendation that had the Beech family goals at the forefront.

During the next family meeting, we presented our collective suggestion. This led to a lengthy discussion and the approval of our recommendation. While the meeting that year lasted three hours, more was accomplished in those three hours than what often takes other families months, even years, to accomplish.

That same year, several other families faced a major decision about whether to give large amounts to their heirs—directly or via a trust—to obtain grandfathering status under a tax benefit that was likely to expire.

Unfortunately, those families weren't as well organized as the Beech family. I know of some who would only meet with their attorney for advice, then get slightly different advice from their accountant, and then another conflicting perspective from someone else on their advisory team. The process was frustrating and counterproductive. In one case, the clients became so fed up, they decided to do nothing! They ended up missing out on an important tax-planning opportunity.

This accentuates the importance for the advisory team to collaborate and reach consensus on what would best serve their client. Not only is it critical for efficiency, but it also gives you as the client peace of mind and confidence that your team is working in your best interest.

Family Disputes After the Second Parent Dies

When the first parent dies, the surviving spouse usually inherits the family assets. This is logical, and under current tax laws it is also tax efficient as there is typically no transfer tax when assets are passed between husband and wife.

Taking care of and focusing on the well-being of the widowed survivor is often priority number one for families. The surviving parent still garners respect in the family and makes family decisions until their death.

But once the surviving parent passes away, crises can develop. Family disputes tend to heat up due to disagreements over the accounting, disposition, and distribution of assets. Unless roles have been defined, relationships are tested and often break down.

If roles have *not* been defined, the children—often middle-aged adults—do not have any experience working together to manage their parents' estate, nor are they accustomed to having hard conversations about the estate. And without practice and defined roles, emotions can run high, often getting in the way of practical decision-making. Before you know it, conflict ensues. Trying to start having effective communication between siblings at that stage is too late.

This stresses the importance of having strong relationships, well-defined roles, and a road map for how to work together, thus avoiding falling into distress like so many families do.

Counselor's Insights

Mark Walsh, the youngest child and only son of Steve and Joanne Walsh, probably felt blindsided by the news his sisters would take on his role as executor of the family estate.

For years, Mark had held this position in the family. He understandably assumed it would translate to the way his parents approached their distribution of assets.

While it wasn't without hiccups, what a blessing that this shift in family roles—and in the bigger family system—took place while their mom and dad were still alive and could influence and stabilize the transition. The family system was able to successfully adjust.

Systems have parts that function in specific ways to maintain the equilibrium—and therefore the predictability—of the system. Weather systems, for example, have identifiable parts that impact and depend on one another. Temperature, pressure, clouds, and moisture are all parts of this system, and a change in one can immediately impact another, leading to a domino effect and a change in the overall system as they are interrelated.

The same is true for the family system.

Whether adaptive or destructive, families naturally yet subconsciously develop roles and patterns, then reinforce those roles and patterns to allow for predictability and stability. And when you consciously assign and develop family roles, your family system can easily adjust and remain stable, even in times of change.

A transfer of wealth is a significant change in the family, which stresses the importance of anticipating and managing the inevitable stress and anxiety that will ensue.

Back to the weather system as an example: the more varied and turbulent the individual components of a weather system, the more varied and turbulent the resulting weather. As temperature, atmospheric pressure, or humidity changes, so does the resulting weather. Huge jumps in one component usually equal a huge shift in the severity of a storm.

The same applies to families. As individuals shift in the role they play in the family—or stop contributing to the system altogether in the case of death—the way in which the family interacts will also change.

The goal is to lessen the inevitable impact on the family system when the leader of the system dies. Already established roles—especially dealing with wealth transfer topics—help to regulate the family system. Getting used to the stabilizing effects of established roles while your parents are still alive and present, helps to alleviate the stress of adjusting and shifting roles someday when they are gone.

Establishing roles while the parents are alive limits the number of factors from changing *simultaneously* in the family system.

In the example of the Walshes, Mark had to shift from leader to support person. Meanwhile, two of his sisters took on leadership roles. But this all happened while their parents were still present. Had the changes not been communicated ahead of time, the family would have had to deal with *three* major changes in the family system at once rather than just with one major change—the death of the parents.

Establishing new roles ahead of time is like avoiding a catastrophic hurricane and getting a thunderstorm instead. It is still a storm, but not nearly as destructive.

Tangible Tools for Defining Roles
- **Be proactive.** Use the stabilizing effect of parents to regulate the system. Invite role-play when trying out potential shifts in roles.
- **Invite creativity to role design.** Listen to and welcome all ideas before narrowing down or eliminating any. Be pleased when your family members are willing to take on a role.
- **Be flexible.** Allow for curiosity and experimentation with family roles, especially in the beginning.
- **Intentionally build in methods to change or adjust roles if needed.** Check in at annual family meetings, asking questions like, "What is the most challenging component

of your role? What do you most enjoy? What do you need support with?"

|||||||||||||

In Short | Without having responsibilities within the family and in the management of an estate, inheritors can feel contemptuous. This is a very strong emotion, which undoubtedly will lead to immense conflict once you're no longer around. Define roles for each person to perform, and practice those while you're still alive. The responsibility that comes with having roles helps each family member feel respected.

Once you are clear about your purpose, your story, your traditions, and your roles, shift the focus to making sure you're promoting a heart of compassion by encouraging humility, the next principle on our list.

5

Promote Humility

There are two ways to live: You can live as if nothing is a miracle, or you can live as if everything is a miracle. The most beautiful thing we can experience is the mysterious. It is the source of all true art and all science. He to whom this emotion is a stranger, who can no longer pause to wonder and stand rapt in awe, is as good as dead; his eyes are closed.
~Albert Einstein

David Wu will never acknowledge the sacrifices his parents, Bo and Mei, had made, nor the tough decisions his sister, Angela, and his brother, John, were forced to make to keep the family business going.

He filed a lawsuit in 2017, suing Angela and John for breach of fiduciary duty.

Principle 5:
Promote Humility
Destructive Emotion:
Selfishness
Constructive Emotion:
Compassion
Proposition:
Celebrate awe and wonder.

David's dividend from the family business had been cut to zero for two straight years, and his lawyer argued that Angela and John Wu were misappropriating funds from the family business.

Had their parents, Bo and Mei, lived to see what transpired between their children from 2017 to 2019, they would have been heartbroken.

Bo and Mei immigrated to the United States in 1953. Their small village in China was still reeling from the impact of the Cultural Revolution, and the young couple—they were in their late 20s—was seeking opportunity for a new life for them and their three small children.

They bought tickets to Newark, New Jersey, knowing just enough English to hail a taxi upon their arrival and head to the tiny apartment friends had secured for them.

Back in his village, Bo had been a laborer. He worked in construction from an early age and knew the ins and outs of the trade. In his words, it was easy to find construction work in the fifties in Newark. It helped that the surrounding suburbs were growing rapidly.

Mei stayed at home with the kids and once told me she learned most of her English watching the *Mickey Mouse Club* with David, Angela, and John. Bo took night classes at church to become fluent in English.

Within five years of landing in New Jersey, Bo found his niche. He saw what companies were paying for plumbing parts and realized there was an opportunity to import materials from China at much lower prices.

In 1958, with a little over $6,000—everything the couple had saved in their first five years in New Jersey—Bo made his first order of plumbing parts, mostly small pipe fittings. He had Mei's full support, but they both acknowledged that they were taking a monumental risk.

Three weeks after submitting the wire transfer, Bo picked up his order at the port of Newark.

Within 10 days he had sold *all* the plumbing parts—at a whopping 200% markup! Even with the huge profit, his prices were less than the other suppliers. Bo and Mei Wu were officially in business. By the end of that year, he quit his laborer job and founded Wu Building Supply, Inc., commonly referred to simply as WBS.

I first met Bo and Mei in 1998 at their office hidden between some New Jersey Turnpike on- and off-ramps—ones I had never taken. Even my GPS got confused trying to get there. New, bigger highways had dwarfed the single-story WBS office and warehouse.

Bo refused to ever sell the office. The distraction and cost of moving were not worth whatever a developer was willing to pay for it.

Driving up, I felt like I was on the pages of Dr. Seuss's story of the Zax:[12]

Well . . . Of course, the world didn't stand still.
The world grew.
In a couple of years, the new highway came through,
And they built it right over those two stubborn Zax
and left them there, standing un-budged in their tracks.

And entering the building, it felt like I had stepped into a time machine. The concrete building was built in 1964. The last time WBS refurbished their office and warehouse was in the late '70s,

---

12 Dr. Seuss. 1961. *The Sneetches and Other Stories*. Random House.

putting in particleboard faux paneling (picture a scene from the *Brady Bunch*) and bright fluorescent lights throughout.

The office reflected a principle that is typical of many first-generation wealth creators: only spend money where necessary.

Bo and Mei had reached out so I could help them update their financial plan. Plus, they were eager to start gifting the WBS stock to their children.

By that time, David had started a music professorship at a major university. His parents had encouraged his love for music from a very young age, and he was truly talented. Bo and Mei were proud to pay for David's education—including two post-graduate degrees—and were very supportive of his career.

As for his younger siblings, Angela and John had started working in the family business immediately after college. They were working their way up the ranks when we met.

Bo and Mei were clear in their wishes: everything was to be shared equally—especially the shares of their largest asset, WBS.

In 2010, Bo and Mei died within just 60 days of each other. From our first meeting in 1998 until their passing, it was inspiring to see the smooth transfer of the company management to Angela as the CEO (chief executive officer) and John as CFO (chief financial officer).

WBS continued growing, and in Bo's final years, he would beam with pride when I'd ask, "How's the family? How's business?"

Mei was concerned, however. She told me, "David's lifestyle is getting too big. He is spending too much money. Why does he need to belong to *three* country clubs?" She went on to say, "He won't listen to me. His priorities are all wrong, and when I bring it up to him, he calls me a nag. Everything is about himself."

David was able to afford this lifestyle because WBS was paying him an after-tax dividend of more than $40,000 per quarter on top of his salary as a professor. He had plenty of extra cash.

During a meeting in the summer of 2015, Angela shared with me real concerns about the company. The year had not started off well, and for the first time in their 57-year history, they projected that WBS would have a year of no profits. She was distraught. They had laid off a third of their employees already with more cuts being necessary.

"New [building-supply] import companies are popping up every day," she told me, "and the US tariffs are killing us."

Angela was concerned about the future of the company and its long-term employees. "I don't know how we can keep going in this environment. Our employees have been so loyal, and I know how much they rely on their paycheck."

I could see the stress it was putting on her.

As projected, that year ended up in the red for WBS. They ended up terminating more than half of their staff, and Angela and John received no bonuses. They cut cash flow everywhere they could—including the termination of shareholder dividends for themselves and their brother David.

David's compassion for the hard work and sacrifice Angela and John put into the company was non-existent. Instead, when they told him the news, he went berserk.

"How could you do this?" David yelled. "Dad sacrificed *everything* for our company. You and John should be ashamed of how you ruined it."

There was no rationalizing with David. He was oblivious to the changes in the business environment and had made up his mind that his siblings were at fault. His dependence on the dividend created a lens that blinded him to the pain his siblings were going through. Instead, he was concerned about how his loss of income would impact his lifestyle. He also had zero empathy for the employees who had lost their jobs.

To say that David was acting selfishly would be an understatement. He refused to see how the challenges WBS was facing far exceeded his hunger for cash.

Within six months, David assembled a legal team that fed this selfishness. Undoubtedly, they played to his fears and convinced him he was right and that he should sue his siblings.

Between 2017 and 2019, the Wu family was at war. David's lawyers relentlessly invaded Angela and John's privacy, digging through their personal tax returns and bank statements. The sparring was unyielding and never-ending.

These events were a huge distraction for an already struggling company, and they created a permanent division between David and his siblings.

In the end, David got what he wanted. The lawsuit was settled for $500,000. In exchange for receiving cash, David's lawyers agreed that David would sell his shares to Angela and John.

Fortunately, Angela and John have since recovered. WBS branched into other building materials, and while smaller, it is back on a growth trajectory. Angela and John continue to be grateful for the opportunity to run the company started by their parents.

||||||||||||

Selfishness is one of the most obvious and most common destructive emotions I have observed in the conflicts arising from an inheritance. When compassion for others is lost, selfishness is the result.

Oscar Wilde captures this well: "Selfishness is not living as one wishes to live. It is asking others to live as one wishes to live."

Belief in a Higher Power

A worldview is a collection of attitudes, values, stories, and expectations about the world. This includes our faith—our belief in a higher power—or our lack of faith. Our worldview informs our every thought and action. Belief in *any* higher power instills a feeling of awe. This, in turn, encourages humility and promotes behaviors opposite of selfishness.

When we realize we are part of something much larger, it changes the way we view money, challenges, and people. It changes the way we view ourselves and all of life!

Identifying your worldview and that of your family members gives you a frame of reference and understanding, especially when challenges arise.

We don't have to see the world in the same way for us to respect each other. However, if we don't *know* each other's worldview, we cannot relate to one another, nor can we connect deeply as a family.

Make a point of talking openly with your children and grandchildren about how they view the world. In doing so, keep an open mind. Even if you don't agree, do what you must to be accepting of each person's worldview.

This is one key to living with humility. As a practicing Catholic, I have found my faith to be a humbling practice, a regular reminder that I am a part of something much larger—a world community. It also reminds me that I am blessed beyond measure and that I can always do more to serve others in need. This is not to say that I never feel selfish or greedy or self-reliant, but regular practice serves as my "humility refresh."

Belief in any higher power and the feeling of awe encourage humility, which promotes behaviors opposite of selfishness. If there is something bigger than us, we as individuals are therefore less important. We are less apt to focus merely on our needs and can see the needs of others and maintain a healthy perspective about ourselves, money, and relationships.

I like Richard Rohr's perspective on humility from his book *Falling Upward*, "In much of urban and Western civilization today. . . we try to believe that it is all upward and onward—all by ourselves."[13]

Rohr goes on to say,

> Almost all of us end up being casualties of this constantly recurring Greek hubris. Some even appear to make it to "the top," but there is usually little recognition of the many shoulders they stood on to move there, the many gratuitous circumstances that made it possible for them to arrive there.[14]

Another favorite perspective on awe and wonder is from Cole Arthur Riley,

> Wonder includes the capacity to be in awe of humanity, even your own. It allows us to jettison the dangerous belief that things worthy of wonder can only be located on nature hikes and scenic overlooks. This can distract us from the beauty flowing through us daily. For every second that our organs

---

13 Richard Rohr. 2011. *Falling Upward: A Spirituality for the Two Halves of Life*. Jossey-Bass.
14 Rohr, *Falling Upward*.

and bones sustain us is a miracle. When those bones heal, when our wounds scab over, this is our call to marvel at our bodies—their regeneration, their stability or frailty. This grows our sense of dignity.[15]

||||||||||||

Belief in a higher power is the second step of Alcoholics Anonymous' 12-step recovery program. As an organization, AA is agnostic—it does not try to convert its members to an individual religion. Their aim with this step is to encourage members to acknowledge that they are powerless against their addiction, that they need a higher power to help them to recovery.

Belief in a higher power is akin to faith or spirituality rather than religion. Faith in a higher power is possible without religious practice.

When we place our faith in something or someone greater than us, it takes the pressure off self-reliance and fear. And fear is the driver of many bad decisions and conflicts.

But sincere belief in a higher power helps encourage life without fear. It allows us to acknowledge we are not in complete control. It also helps us realize we are not alone and helps us find purpose.

||||||||||||

In addition to finding purpose in a higher power, there's another element that significantly impacts our worldview, our sense of

---

[15] Cole Arthur Riley. 2022. *This Here Flesh: Spirituality, Liberation, and the Stories That Make Us.* Convergent Books.

purpose, and our most important motivations. It's what Sigmund Freud called the id—the unconscious component of personality that forms the basis of our most primitive impulses.

The id drives the desire for immediate gratification and engaging in other fun or potentially harmful behaviors, often at the cost of doing more productive activities. The id also drives our urge for survival and, in the face of fear or insecurity, causes us to act selfishly.

Several of the interviews that I had with inheritors with successful transitions of wealth spoke about these themes of destructive and selfish behaviors. Their responses to these behaviors had this in common: in one form or another, they all practiced daily gratitude and acknowledgment of a higher power. These families also spoke of humility as a characteristic they saw in their parents and family.

One family member described belief in a higher power in his family as awe: wonder and reverence when overwhelmed by the presence of something beautiful and inspiring.

When was the last time you felt awe? Was it in witnessing the birth of a child, experiencing death with a loved one, or being in nature—seeing the Rocky Mountains, the red rock formations of Sedona, or the vastness of space on a clear night for the first time?

These are the jaw-dropping experiences where we can appreciate how small, and insignificant, we are as individuals.

Another antidote to selfishness is to serve others. Serving others, especially in an environment outside our comfort zone, can likewise instill awe. (We'll look more at that in the next chapter.) It also instills humility.

Encourage awe as part of your estate plan. Share your belief in a higher power as a standard and a priority for your beneficiaries.

Consider an awe-filled vacation experience that provides a view into nature, or impact to a community in the area you are visiting.

Models of Humility

"They are as comfortable dining with kings as they are with paupers." That is how Anne Mallon described her parents, now in their late 70s. John and Mary Mallon are generous with their time and money. They are dedicated to their church and helping a struggling community in Honduras.

When I sat down with Anne, I asked if her parents had always been this way. She told me that her dad grew up in a plumbing business with his dad. He used to scrub the bricks at their office on his hands and knees with his bare hands. John eventually took over the family business. This provided great monetary wealth to the family.

As for Mary, she came from modest means with faith and family being in the forefront of her life. She is a lifelong Democrat, while John favors Republican views. Despite their differences, their relationship works. In Anne's words, her parents' relationship is "unified, but not uniform—like many families are."

Their work in Honduras was inspired during their first trip to Central America, when they observed extreme poverty firsthand. That trip changed their lives.

Over decades and numerous trips back to Honduras, the Mallons have helped to establish a sister church and have provided immeasurable support to families in that church community.

But these aren't things their children or grandchildren would necessarily know. So, each Christmas, the Mallons attach two envelopes to their Christmas tree for their grandchildren. One has a letter outlining the contribution they made that year to the kids' college fund, accentuating the importance of education. The other outlines the donations they made that year to the village in Honduras, stressing the value of charity.

Anne told me that she has felt blessed throughout her life. But early on in high school, she had an experience that brought perspective on her family wealth. She visited a friend's home in a trailer park. This home was *much* different than the Mallon house!

Also, when it came time to choose colleges, Anne remembered how while she could choose any school she could get into, many of her classmates had only a *short* list of schools they could choose from—schools that their families could afford.

To Anne, these experiences were sobering.

After college, Anne had the opportunity to work in Costa Rica for a year. This, along with several other trips abroad during her childhood and young-adult years provided a sense of awe and of gratitude for her family's wealth. It also instilled in her a deep sense of compassion.

Anne, now in her 50s, shared that her parents have consistently modeled perspective to their children and grandchildren. She identified three core philosophies learned from her parents, ones that she and her husband are working hard to pass along:

1. **Live a good life.** How you define a good life is entirely based on your perspective—your worldview. And how you view life informs your values.
2. **Develop unique gifts and talents.** It's crucial to identify what your unique gifts and talents are. Of equal importance is to notice how different your talents are from those of your parents and your children and to be willing to support gifts and talents that differ from yours.
3. **Leverage gifts and talents for the benefit of others.** Be a conduit. Do not hold on to your gifts and talents for

yourself. Not recognizing a gift is like throwing it back and declaring, "This isn't good enough!"

The Mallons have yet to experience an intergenerational transfer of wealth, but with the example of their parents instilling belief in a higher power, serving as stewards of wealth, and emphasizing those in need, their family has a grace-filled and rational perspective on wealth. Plus, the children and grandchildren have seen firsthand what living with humility looks like.

The Importance of Humility

Humility isn't the most appealing of all virtues. So asserts Dr. Anna Schaffner, pointing out that the word comes from *humus*, the Greek word for earth. Humility, Schaffner says,

> . . . appears to clash with our current valuation of self-worth and self-realization. But humility has nothing to do with meekness or weakness. And neither does it mean being self-effacing or submissive.
>
> Humility is an attitude of spiritual modesty that comes from understanding our place in the larger order of things. It entails not taking our desires, successes, or failings too seriously.
>
> In the past decade in particular, psychologists have rediscovered the importance of humility. They have established fascinating links between humility and our ability to learn and be effective leaders, and our readiness to engage in pro-social behavior.
>
> Adopting a more humble mindset increases our overall psychological well-being and ensures our social functioning.

> Last but not least, humility is a perfect antidote to the self-fixated spirit of our age.[16]

||||||||||||

Humility typically isn't the first thing we as parents strive to promote in our children. Instead, we have a universal goal: *we want what is best for our children.* We want them to live a healthy, comfortable, and fulfilling life. And we're willing to sacrifice almost everything to support them in getting there.

But facing challenges and even failing are necessary parts of growing up. Making things too easy for our children and solving their problems for them robs them of whatever lessons can be learned from the experience.

The long-term manifestation of a coddled upbringing is adults whose emotional maturity has been stifled. They are selfish, motivated by security, success, and image. Their hunger for more and more of each of these elements is insatiable.

At its worst, such an obsession with security, financial success, and outward appearance can lead to mental instability and a win-at-all-costs mentality. Such individuals think nothing of bending the rules, taking excessive risks, and taking advantage of others.

Unfortunately, if Wall Street had a Hall of Shame, it would be riddled with examples of people creating disastrous outcomes from their fixation on financial success. The most notable example? Bernie Madoff. He stole more than $20 billion from individuals and pension funds. Harvard Business School Professor Eugene Soltes did a series of phone interviews with Madoff asking him,

---

[16] Anna Katharina Schaffner, PhD. "What Is Humility & Why Is It Important?" Positive Psychology.com. October 19, 2023.

among other questions, "How would you explain your actions and misconduct to students?"

Madoff said, "I sort of rationalized that what I was doing was OK, that it wasn't going to hurt anybody." And, "I built my confidence up to a level where I . . . felt that . . . there was nothing that . . . I couldn't attain."[17]

A Need for Security

As in the case of Madoff, those who lack compassion see the world only as what's in it for *them*. And when that's the lens through which they see the world, they will not only be selfish, but they may also have a scarcity mentality. There's just never enough. They become obsessed with financial security. And people obsessed with not having enough often become hoarders.

Hoarding can look like someone having a home where they can barely get around mountains of clutter. (A&E Network's *Hoarders* has been taking viewers behind the scenes since 2009 as families, friends, and experts intervene to help their loved ones reclaim their space and, with it, their lives.) But that's just one way an obsession with security shows up.

Hoarding can also present as someone with money in a trust fund who is obsessed with getting the assets into their own name, often against the trust creator's original intent—even to the point of hiring lawyers to sue the trustee.

It can also present as someone who has plenty of money, yet they believe they need more and more and more!

A Harvard Business School study of individuals with more than $8 million in assets underscores this. (In March 2018, *Money*

---

[17] Carmen Nobel, "Bernie Madoff Explains Himself," Harvard Business School, October 24, 2016, https://hbswk.hbs.edu/item/bernie-madoff-explains-himself

magazine ran an article on these findings under the title "The Insane Amount Millionaires Say They Need to Be Happy.")[18]

According to a Harvard study, 25% of the respondents insisted they needed five times more money—at least $40 million—before they would describe themselves as happy, with a further 27% of respondents saying they'd need *ten* times more money—$80 million—to be happy. Sadly, only 13% said they were happy with what they had.[19]

Perhaps the most troubling statistic from the study is that those who earned their wealth were statistically happier than those who inherited it.

⁂

Yet another way a need for security can show up as is an obsession with image. Such folks buy stuff they don't need—excessive amounts of clothing or all the latest gadgets. Among those with more disposable income, this extends to high-dollar obsessions such as cars and vacation properties. Much of this can purely be for their "personal brand" or for the sake of appearance rather than addressing an actual need.

Among second- and third-generation inheritors, I have also observed folks collecting memberships to country clubs, golf clubs, or social clubs with high initiation fees and annual dues.

I have had several inheritors confide that although they haven't been to a particular club in years, they keep paying the dues sim-

---

18   Kristen Bahler. "The Insane Amount Millionaires Say They Need to Be Happy." *Money Magazine*. December 20, 2017.
19   Grant E. Donnelly, Tianyi Zheng, Emily Haisley & Michael I. Norton. "The Amount and Source of Millionaires' Wealth (Moderately) Predicts Their Happiness." *Personality & Social Psychology Bulletin*. 44(5). January 11, 2018.

ply so they can *say* they are a member. To me, these behaviors further stress the importance of the principles outlined in this book.

Counselor's Insights

In the Wu family story, there was a definitive lack of intention to inspire humility. But that was not the only contributing factor to David's determination to receive what he claimed to be his fair share, nor the conflict that resulted.

It's easy to empathize with the Wus' focus on survival as first-generation immigrants. They would have experienced awe by watching their children succeed in education and creative exploration—something they never could have imagined for themselves. As for humility, though, it's a challenge to promote when you've fought your whole life to be lifted from a humble situation.

As a therapist drawn to an internal family systems (IFS) framework of thinking, the notion of *self* is key to the process of therapeutic healing and sustained mental and relational health.

Richard Schwartz, who developed the concept of IFS, describes self as an innate, internal leader that possesses the eight qualities of curiosity, clarity, calm, creativity, courage, confidence, connectedness, and compassion.[20]

The concept of self isn't new. It has been called many names in different cultures—inner light, true self, the third eye, and more.

I would encourage you to view *any* resource that helps you tap into yourself and inspires the eight qualities of self as a "higher power." For it is when you embody even a fraction of one or more

---

[20] Richard C. Schwartz. 2021. *No Bad Parts: Healing Trauma & Restoring Wholeness with the Internal Family Systems Model.* Sounds True.

of the eight characteristics listed that you'll be tapping into the state of heart necessary for a peaceful succession of wealth. And when you lead with curiosity, compassion, and creativity, you'll stand a much better chance at maintaining connection, which is key to a smooth transition.

I had the pleasure of listening to Tom Holmes speak at the IFS Institute's annual conference in 2023, and some of what he said pertains here.

Holmes invited us to view "higher power" as an external representation of the inner burning flame of self. Those are connected and related in some way. The two can be beautifully tied and integrated.

Religion or any intentional spiritual practice, meanwhile, can be likened to a shield with which you protect the flame from being blown out by any disturbance coming its way. Its structure, ritual, sacraments, or traditions help provide that framework of protection.

But if a structure is *too* tight, you risk snuffing out your flame and even the flames of those around you. Conversely, a shield or framework that is too loose or non-existent will make your flame vulnerable to being blown out by even small disturbances in the environment.

I encourage you to reinforce curiosity, clarity, calm, creativity, courage, confidence, connectedness, and compassion.

Promote these, and awe will naturally follow. And where awe lives, humility lives.

Tangible Tools for Promoting Humility

- **Experiment with your family's personal expression and cultivation of awe.** If a religious framework was passed down to you from previous generations, discuss with your

spouse and children how you can make it your own by incorporating updated traditions and family rituals.
- **Solidify your shield of choice.** If you have pursued awe outside a formal framework, name it, then schedule those experiences, thus strengthening your shield. For example, being in nature can be awe inspiring. Try a monthly "time to notice nature" walk where everyone picks up at least one piece of litter. This encourages humility and respect for our planet.
- **Always invite creativity and curiosity** into your family's pursuit of awe. Welcome all ideas and approaches.
- **Model humility.** Acknowledge that no one owns—or has exclusive domain over—the pursuit of awe.

|||||||||||||

In Short | If spiritual modesty is not already part of your family culture, consider using awe and wonder to stimulate compassion. Recognizing your place in the larger order of things will influence future behavior and deter selfishness.

So far, we've covered more than half of the principles: develop a common purpose, share your story, forge traditions, define roles, and promote humility. Next, we'll look at how nurturing independence can further support your quest to bequeath *the greatest gift*.

6

Nurture Independence

You have to do your own growing no matter how tall your grandfather was.
~Abraham Lincoln

The Cook family has been in the concrete business for generations. The combination of four simple ingredients—limestone, clay, sand, and water—has made them *very* wealthy!

What started in mid-state Pennsylvania in the early 1930s as a company providing concrete blocks for construction, has grown into a multi-state empire.

In 1997, I met Sandra, Jamie, and Michael, members of the third generation of the Cook family business. The day I made the three-hour drive from my office to meet them at their con-

Principle 6:
Nurture Independence
Destructive Emotion:
Enmeshment
Constructive Emotion:
Independence
Proposition:
Growth needs space.

crete plant, the sky was clear after some morning rains, and the fall foliage was in full glory, the colors of the autumn leaves calming during the long drive.

When we met, their parents had recently passed and left trusts of more than $10 million each for the three adult children.

The trusts had been set up to be generation-skipping, meaning that Sandra, Jamie, and Michael would receive income distributions for their lifetimes—more than $300,000 each for life. The principal, however, was intended to be passed to their children.

If there was a need for additional support for healthcare or other emergencies, the trustee had the discretion to invade the principal to make special distributions. But if these heirs could live off the income each year and not dip into the trust corpus, their children would not have to pay inheritance tax on the $10 million.

Sandra and I met privately a few weeks after that initial meeting. She filled me in on some additional details, including that she and her siblings were all college-educated, and that she and Michael had established themselves with careers in consulting and publishing.

But Jamie and her husband were comfortable living off her trust distribution. In Sandra's words, Jamie had "never worked a day in her life and her sole mission was to break the terms of the trust and get the money distributed to herself."

The estate also determined that the three siblings would own a vacation home together. I had the privilege of visiting the home during one of our initial meetings. It was a modest cottage about 45 minutes north of the factory—situated less than 100 feet from a picturesque trout stream. Nestled amidst the overhanging trees with a background of gurgling water, this was a perfect spot for a family meeting.

At the time of our initial meeting, all was well between the siblings. But a mere two years after the death of their parents, the three were fighting over the fair use and fair contribution to the upkeep of the cottage.

Jamie and her family were using it most frequently since they had no career obligations. Sandra only used the home on holidays (that is, if Jamie and her family weren't there). And Michael lived far enough away that he never used the property.

Still, Jamie felt she should only pay a third of the upkeep, repair, and utility expenses. Michael and Sandra disagreed. They argued the utilities needed to be split based on use. They also argued that the home needed to be rented for at least two months per year to help offset these expenses, but Jamie vehemently disagreed.

A solution to the problem of ownership and shared expenses was to sell the property. Sandra and Michael wanted to sell it outright, but Jamie threatened to hold up any sale indefinitely. She wanted her trust to buy it.

Arguments ensued. Jamie felt it was fair and right for her to buy the home since it had been their parents' vacation home. Plus, her family had made many memories there.

Eventually, Sandra and Michael agreed to sell the home to Jamie, but the price would be based upon a third-party valuation, which ended up being higher than Jamie thought was fair. She was willing to pay only 80% of the valuation price.

After months of heartbreaking disagreement and conflict, Sandra and Michael decided that making peace was more valuable than continuing to argue. They were ready to let go of the stress and fissure being created by Jamie's stubbornness.

They agreed to sell the property to Jamie's trust at the discounted price. Still, the arguments and insults that led up to the resolution created permanent scars on the family. Sandra and

Michael had not talked to Jamie for years, and their children have been effectively cut off from their cousins.

What's more, not long after Jamie's trust purchased the vacation home, the trustee let me know that Jamie had hired a lawyer to sue the trustees to disband her trust and distribute the principal. While her parents had envisioned passing their wealth and providing education and healthcare for their grandchildren and beyond, Jamie's lack of independence and personal aspirations robbed her children of that gift.

Not only that; it has also created unbelievable conflict at the expense of all the heirs to the Cook fortune.

Shirtsleeves to Shirtsleeves . . .?

"Shirtsleeves to shirtsleeves in three generations" is a quote attributed to Andrew Carnegie. There is also the Scottish equivalent: "The father buys, the son builds, the grandchild sells, and his son begs." Both describe the challenge of maintaining family wealth. It represents Jamie's focus on spending the trust corpus at the expense of her children's inheritance.

I believe Jamie's priority stemmed from being dependent on her parents' wealth. Meanwhile, her brother and sister formed a healthy relationship with money and the trust assets over time. They created lives independent of the trust assets, allowing them to concentrate on the *stewardship* of the family trust assets versus the *spending* thereof.

There are plenty of stories to back up the shirtsleeves quote, but little data to prove it. Josh Baron and Rob Lachenauer wrote an article published in the *Harvard Business Review* in which the authors challenged the validity of the "shirtsleeves to shirtsleeves" adage.[21]

Many multi-generational family businesses that succeed are privately held, and there are few reliable statistics on the longevity of such companies. Instead, the information is kept confidential. Those families that succeed across multiple generations contradict the shirtsleeves adage through careful stewardship and education.

Conversely, a study published by the *Journal of the Royal Society* looked at 25,000 publicly traded companies from 1950 to 2009 and found that, on average, *publicly traded* companies lasted only around 15 years, not even through a single generation.[22] (The longevity of a business can be a misleading measure, though. In this study, companies that were acquired by others are considered having gone out of existence.)

We often only hear about the family businesses that fail or have terrible conflict, especially the ones that sensationally fall from grace. Often, the failure is that of character, not a failure of the business.

Consider the Redstone family whose succession was publicly debated between 2006 until the death of Sumner Redstone in 2020. Sumner's daughter Shari and he had regular spats made public by their spokespeople.[23]

Likewise, the Gucci empire saw its second-generation inheritor Aldo Gucci, the "ambassador of fashion," serve prison time for

---

21 Josh Baron & Rob Lachenauer. "Do Most Family Businesses Really Fail by the Third Generation?" Harvard Business School. July 19, 2021.
22 Madeleine I. G. Daepp, Marcus J. Hamilton, Geoffrey B. West & Luís M. A. Bettencourt. "The Mortality of Companies." *Journal of Royal Society.* May 6, 2015. 12(106)
23 Eller, C. and Hiltzik, M.A., "Redstone's Letter Takes Public Slap at Daughter," *Los Angeles Times*, July 21, 2007

tax evasion, only to be followed by a hostile takeover by his son and nephew.[24]

Successful intergenerational transfer takes intention. Meaningful planning for assets, education, communication, and emotional grounding is necessary. And this takes forethought on the part of the parents.

Accept Differences

Intentionality goes beyond planning for the transfer of assets, though. It extends to—or possibly starts with—relationships among family members. While this seems obvious, maintaining strong relationships is not always that easy. Especially when a child or grandchild has a lifestyle that is different than yours.

Your family's balance sheet—your net worth—is an easy measurement of wealth. It is the default. Some even refer to it as their scorecard.

But prosperity is not measured only in dollars.

There is no standard measurement of the other non-monetary elements of wealth: health, knowledge, wisdom, courage, counsel, service, healing, intelligence, beauty, morality, leadership, craftsmanship, and relational wealth.

Every person has value—even those who have interests, talents, personalities, perspectives, and lifestyles that are different than ours. Celebrating such differences demonstrates more than just acceptance. It demonstrates unconditional love.

Celebrating our differences and finding each person's unique talents are also some of the best ways to encourage personal devel-

---

24 Lubasch, A.H., "Gucci, 81, Gets Year in Prison in Federal Tax Case," *New York Times*, September 12, 1986

opment. How talents show up, as well as how they're fostered, is part of each person's life journey.

For many—including me—encouraging and celebrating diversity take effort. For example, as a "numbers guy" with zero musical blood in my veins, it scared me when our daughter Kylie chose songwriting as her college major. It was hard for me to see a pathway to financial independence in this field.

I was determined to convince Kylie to pick a degree with a clear pathway to a solid job in a less crowded industry. Thankfully, Jill talked me out of doing that. She helped me see the importance of supporting Kylie and her musical talents.

Kylie's passion for writing was clear. By the time she was applying for colleges, she had already created enough content to fill multiple notebooks.

By the time she was ready to choose her college and major, it was easy for us to be sincere when we gave our support to her and her passion for songwriting. And while she had our backing and we wanted to nurture her individuality, we also reminded Kylie that we expected a full-time commitment to her craft, and that becoming financially self-sufficient was not optional. Just like with her brothers, we'd expect her to support herself once she graduates.

We also want Kylie to *love* her job someday, and that means allowing her to pursue her passion.

||||||||||||

I'll never forget the empty feeling just after college of being in a job I didn't like. Even though I worked at a great hotel group, I didn't love what I was doing. That's when my Uncle George gave me a chance at a new career path.

Years later, I saw the same happen to my sister Jenny. After graduating college, Jenny worked as a pharmaceutical representative. She is an amazing person, has the most wonderful, engaging personality, and she is easy to be around. So, when she said she wanted to move closer to home, my brother Mike and I jumped at the opportunity to recruit her to work at Valley Forge.

We decided Jenny would become my trainee. Before she started, I let Jenny know the first 12 months would be the hardest. "Just hang in there for the first year," I told her, "and then you'll find your rhythm."

Studying for exams and licenses, learning best practices with clients, and getting used to waking up early and driving—*a lot*—to see clients are big adjustments. Eleven months in, Jenny resigned. She had stayed as long as she could stand it.

Jenny was afraid that Mike and I would be upset, but we weren't. We wanted her to be happy! She went back to school and became a nurse. And she is an *awesome* nurse—the best there is.

I like to remind her that those 11 months at Valley Forge were very important in her journey. They helped her see what she did *not* like doing for work! It also makes me feel less guilty about recruiting her in the first place.

In a post on Medium.com titled "How to Boldly Find Your Place in the World When You Don't Know How," Dr. Eugene Choi writes, "All individuals have a burning desire within themselves and a unique set of skills that can help create a meaningful impact on the world, but until we take the time to intimately connect with culture and cultivate them, we will never find our true calling."[25]

---

25 Eugene Choi. "How to Boldly Find Your Place in the World When You Don't Know How." Medium.com. May 19, 2018.

The trap of the phrase *true calling* is the potential for constant dissatisfaction.

We all know folks who get multiple graduate degrees—not out of a desire to learn and contribute to research, but because college life is appealing. Likewise, there are those who are constantly changing jobs or moving from city to city, always discontent with what they have, always in search of the "perfect job" or the "perfect life."

I'm not saying accepting differences is about encouraging this type of unsettled behavior. It's about being patient and supportive, within a reasonable time frame, until they find their niche.

Dr. Choi goes on to say, "Your calling isn't always about what you are doing, but it has everything to do with *what you are becoming*."

Did you catch that? Your children's or grandchildren's calling is about more than just their career choice. It's about who they're becoming in the process.

It's worth paying attention to whether they have a natural aptitude or skill for something, or a natural talent for certain subjects in school.

Ask them about it. Ask them what they see themselves doing, and who they see themselves becoming. Use your resources not only to encourage their talent, but also to support them in healing if healing is what they need, or in therapy if that's what they need.

As you deepen your relationship through listening and supporting them, also be clear about what you expect from them *and* what they can expect from you—both monetarily and emotionally. It's all crucial in their development.

And remember: their true worth isn't expressed in numbers.

Parenting for Success

In her book, *Raised Healthy, Wealthy & Wise*, author Coventry Edwards-Pitt shares real-world examples of successful inheritors, stories of failure and hard work that helped form their sense of self.

The author stresses the importance of natural consequences, accountability, discipline, and empowerment as critical elements to self-actualization. And she shares the common thread among successful, happy inheritors being the *intentional shaping of their character* and perspective on the role of financial assets in their life.

Specifically, she found that successful children who demonstrate an ability to earn their own money are motivated toward achieving personal goals, have a solid sense of self, and can overcome setbacks.

Edwards-Pitt concludes, "We realized that the families with the most successful children—young adults who are financially and emotionally independent of their parents—were conveying similar core messages to their children."[26]

Clients often ask for resources on how to teach their children about money. Those who ask are often in a more secure financial position than the environment in which they were raised. These clients aren't necessarily ultra-wealthy, but they are financially secure.

Most of them didn't grow up with a model or an example of how to work with money. Their parents were too busy focusing on paying the monthly bills and making ends meet. They didn't talk to their kids about money or concepts of financial management.

And for these clients, earning their own money was natural during their formative years. If parents weren't providing cash or a

---

[26] Coventry Edwards-Pitt. 2014. *Raised Healthy, Wealthy & Wise: Lessons from Successful and Grounded Inheritors on How They Got that Way.* Coventry Edwards-Pitt.

spending allowance for clothing, let alone a car, they found ways to make money. They sought financial independence for themselves.

Edwards-Pitt's notion of encouraging children to earn their own money seems so basic. Yet a typical pattern might go like this: parents who fought for financial independence want to provide a smooth pathway for their children by giving them a spending allowance and supporting their every need. And this removes the need for a child to earn their own money.

If you think back on your first job, though, you might recall the many lessons you learned about yourself, about others, and about life.

Consider how providing a smooth pathway for your children can easily backfire with you essentially robbing your children and grandchildren of the confidence that real, hard life experience provides.

Parenting isn't easy. My father-in-law likes to say that it's like a giant experiment. With each child, we learn what works and what doesn't work for that child.

Deliberate emphasis on natural consequences, accountability, discipline, and empowerment are keys to success. As is allowing children to fail.

Building Character Through Failure

One of the goals of successful parenting is to raise kids who can make it on their own. Fail at this and you have offspring who rely on you well into adulthood. Even worse, you raise kids whose behavior is marked by enmeshment and codependence—the opposite of independence.

For purposes of this discussion, enmeshment happens when children grow up with poorly defined or nonexistent relational boundaries. Other than building strong ties with a parent, such kids often struggle with friendships. Instead, enmeshed children heavily rely on their parents and struggle with being independent. And someone who is codependent has problems making decisions on their own. They likely also struggle with being in interdependent relationships.

In both these cases, a child may need support in learning how to build relationships, solve problems, and make decisions.

Enmeshment and codependence can also show up as entitlement, being loathsome, and being problematic—not the picture of the independent heirs you would want to entrust with an inheritance.

One of several ways in which you can foster independence and growth is by giving your heirs the permission and opportunity to fail.

||||||||||||

Character is built in many ways, including through failure and the recovery from failure. In fact, how you recover from failure is often seen as a measure of character.

For this reason, it's crucial to challenge and allow your heirs to fail rather than always be there to protect them. This way, they can learn from their failures.

Share with them what you have learned from your own failures too. Let them know how failure—and the recovery from failure—has shaped you and impacted your life.

My children have taught me the importance of failure firsthand. All three of them have been competitive swimmers. Originally, Jill and I enrolled them in swimming to help them burn excess energy. As they matured, competitive swimming taught them the importance of consistent hard work, goal setting, and resilience.

When they were successful, we celebrated together. And when their performance at competitions was disappointing or they missed goals—even by tenths or hundredths of a second—we shared their heartache.

As a freshman in high school, our son Ryan had one goal for the year: make the YMCA national qualification time in the 100 meter butterfly. Ryan had high hopes for making the team and joining his older brother and teammates at the national meet in North Carolina.

But first, he had to make the cut at the district championship.

At nationals, he'd be competing against the best of the best at a four-day meet in North Carolina. It also meant missing a few days of school. It was a rite of passage for a young swimmer, and it meant everything to Ryan that year.

But the season ended with tears.

Districts were held at LaSalle University in Philadelphia, as they had always been. The LaSalle pool was a familiar place for all of us. My dad is a graduate of LaSalle, and I swam at the same pool back when I was Ryan's age!

It's an old indoor pool with lots of spectator seating on both sides of the deck. The ceiling is high enough to accommodate a three-meter diving board in the separate diving well. The spectator area is dark, but the lighting is bright over the pool as if it were stage lights in a Broadway theater.

Coming into the meet, Ryan was just a few tenths of a second away from the qualifying time for nationals, but he was confident he would make it. After all, he had been training and preparing like his life depended on it. During warm-up, Ryan said his body felt ready and his stroke felt strong.

Jill and I sat nervously in the stands as Ryan's race started. Knowing how much qualifying would mean to him, we wanted him to make it more than anything.

Ryan's stroke looked great, but in the final 10 meters, we could see him tightening up. Every muscle in his back and upper arms was tense. This was slowing him down.

The moment he touched the end of the pool, Ryan whipped his head around to check the clock. He missed the cut by less than a few hundredths of a second! It was of little consolation to him that he received the silver medal in the district for his age group.

On the way home, I marveled at Jill's ability to console our son. "I can see how heartbroken you are to not achieve the goal you've worked so very hard for . . ." she told Ryan. "Even given your incredible effort and the amazing time you made, coming in second in the district, no less, I know it still wasn't what you hoped for. That's disappointing. Just know, we love watching you compete, Ryan. You're *such* a talented swimmer! You'll get the cut, it's just a matter of when . . . And I know you'll enjoy the ride getting there."

Lots of tears and hugs later, Ryan moved on. But the experience at districts became his daily motivation to push when it hurt—to work even harder during his sophomore year. In addition to after-school practices every day, he elected to train several mornings a week.

That year, Ryan made the national qualifying time in the 100 meter butterfly even before the mid-season meet. He crushed it by over a second. He also made national cuts in two other events. By the end of that year, he could see his freshman-year experience for what it was—continued preparation for his future success. What a valuable lesson it was for him.

While our children were younger, what Jill and I often didn't realize was the long-lasting impact lessons such as these provided for life long after events like competitive swimming were over.

As much as we might hate failing, we need failure to get better. Failure teaches us invaluable lessons. It helps us develop emotionally. And it helps us develop grit.

Competitive sports provide a failure-recovery-success cycle in a safe environment. Athletes might be devastated after a bad competition or a loss, but it's temporary. Recovery is possible and expected of athletes. Success usually follows. It comes from more practice, more discipline, and more work. This is a healthy pattern to inspire as it will be reinforced and required in later stages of life.

This failure-recovery-success cycle also applies in all long-term avocations. Encourage your children and grandchildren to participate in various environments where they can fail, recover, and succeed—sports, music, art, song, dance, and chess all provide a forum for impressing the importance and comfort of failure, and more importantly, the recovery from failure.

Having financial resources makes it tempting to always provide a smooth path for our children—to fix whatever is broken or provide an out. Resources can be used to help prevent failure. While this may be well intended, protecting children from failure deprives them from learning how to recover when they inevitably meet challenges later in life.

If they are struggling in school, we could either blame the teacher or recognize that our child might need help improving their study habits.

If a child doesn't want to go to practice for a sport or a music or art lesson, we could back down and let them skip, or we could encourage them to persevere even when they're tired.

When a child gets in trouble, we could use our connections to get them out of it, or we can let them face the natural consequences of their behavior.

Our oldest son, Zach, had a frustrating time finding his first job out of college. Throughout his senior year, he searched and searched for his perfect job. He attended countless job fairs and had several interviews without finding the right fit.

Zach received an offer from a small company that would allow him to be self-sufficient, but it didn't check all the boxes for him. Jill and I could see the toll it was taking on our son. As graduation approached, many of his friends already had their dream jobs. Zach admitted feeling like a failure, and panic was starting to set in.

Finally, with amazing timing—on the last day of finals—Zach received the job offer he wanted.

To be honest, with Zach being our oldest, Jill and I had no experience launching a child. We had a network and resources and were very tempted to make things easier for him. We even had several conversations about where Zach might fit at my company and talked about if there was a way to start a business for him to run. Thankfully, we decided not to follow through on those thoughts and instead let him find his own way.

Zach proved his tenacity. He was patient and held out until he received the offer he wanted. I attribute his doggedness in the job search to his years and years of competitive sports.

In the hard times during his senior year of college, he may have felt like a failure, but deep down, he knew he would find the right opportunity with continued networking and interviews.

About a year after Zach started his job, I read *Willing Wisdom* by Thomas William Deans. Deans writes, "The more inherited money eclipses earned money, the more despondent and damaged the recipient's psyche can become, [and] the more inheritance can rob and undermine their true sense of self."[27]

---

[27] Thomas William Deans. 2013. *Willing Wisdom*. Detente Financial Press, Ltd.

The quote catches the essence of our philosophy with Zach's job search. Deep down, we knew giving Zach a job would have stolen his sense of self and robbed him of the satisfaction of finding a job on his own.

Said differently, inheriting money, being given a job, or being set up with a job is not in itself gratifying. It doesn't lead to happiness. Without development of character and a real sense of independence, how can we expect true happiness for our loved ones?

The Pressure of a Name

An inheritor of a fourth-generation family business once told me, "Imagine going through life with people thinking they know who you are because of your last name . . ."

His family name is known throughout the world. Their name is on buildings. Movies have been made about his relatives.

And until this conversation, I didn't fully appreciate the difficulty of defining oneself and shaping an individual personality when being raised in a wealthy and notable family.

His comment gave me a deep sense of empathy for the burden he has carried. His motivation for starting several businesses seems to have come from a need to prove to others that he is smart and capable—not just an heir to a fortune.

I admit falling prey to judgment of people with recognizable names. I once met a prospective client with a notable generational family name. The person who introduced me said, "She'll be a great client and definitely needs your help. She's a . . ." and mentioned the person's last name.

As it turns out, she *was* a wonderful person, but she had absolutely no ties to the notable family or its tremendous fortune. I would imagine you may have had this experience too—assuming we know a person or their character simply because we know their last name.

This was not the first time someone's reputation was described to me simply by using their name, nor will it be the last.

But the pressure of your name can come from non-financial reasons too. The father of a friend of ours was a legendary high-school football coach. Whenever our friend is back in town, folks simply call him "Coach Jim's son." I suspect this lack of folks seeing our friend for who he is—not just for who his *dad* was—might be one of the reasons he moved out of state.

Remember: *your last name is not your character.* Your name doesn't reflect who you are, nor who your children and grandchildren are. While you legitimately would want them to do you proud, you'll also want them to make it on their own.

|||||||||||||

The legendary investor and founder of Berkshire Hathaway, Warren Buffett, has been very public about his views on inheritance. He has pledged most of his wealth to charity upon his death. He emphasizes the total value of the person—not only their total dollar net worth.

It appears his strategy is working. Warren's son Peter wrote a book called, *Life Is What You Make It: Find Your Own Path to Fulfillment.* In it, he says, "No matter who your parents are, you've still got your own life to figure out."[28]

When he was interviewed on National Public Radio in 2010, Buffett said there are many assumptions that come with being his

---

28 Peter Buffett. 2010. *Life Is What You Make It: Find Your Own Path to Fulfillment.* Crown Publishing Group.

father's son, mainly an easy life of money and privilege. But as this quote from the conversation on NPR shows, Warren Buffett and his wife, Susan, offered their children far more than money:

> But the support—the privilege, really—comes from having two parents that said and believed that I could do anything. That support didn't come in the form of a check. That support came in the form of love and nurturing and respect for us finding our way, falling down, figuring out how to get up ourselves.[29]

The challenge is to raise individuals who have their own personality and character separate from their parents and grandparents. This is especially challenging for children of famous, notable, and notorious families.

Be deliberate and aware of the shadow cast by your family name. Be careful not to confuse identity with name. Your children's identity must be defined by their core values and their talents.

An Emphasis on Personal Strengths

As you may recall from the earlier story about my Uncle George and Aunt Karen, my brother and I purchased our financial-services company from my aunt and cousins. This makes us second-generation business owners.

Some folks assume we inherited the business and would comment on how nice that must be. That has made me work even harder to prove that I earned my leadership position; it wasn't handed to me on a silver platter.

---

29 National Public Radio, Morning Edition. "Buffett's Lasting Legacy: Immaterial Wealth." https://bit.ly/buffett-legacy. May 6, 2010.

For others who do, in fact, inherit a family business—whether a mom-and-pop shop or a booming business—I can see why it would be intimidating to work at, or take over a family business when it's not aligned with your interests or natural skill set. Yet this pattern is repeated over and over again in many a family business.

Too often, I have observed children taking their first job at the family company out of convenience. In PwC's 2021 "Family Business Survey," a survey of approximately 2,800 decision-makers in 87 territories, almost two-thirds of family businesses surveyed desired to have next-generation family members working in the company.[30, 31]

I have observed a pattern among several inheritors who have chosen to rebel against family wealth and the family business. Consciously or not, some disassociate with their parents and family members.

I have seen cases where children moved out of the country, purposely dressed in tattered clothes, and even took on an imaginary personality as if the family and its wealth did not exist. All of this is done to create independence that was not otherwise fostered in their upbringing.

―――――――――

If you have a family business, consider a policy where family members must attain a certain level of education or first work elsewhere for some time. In a *Harvard Business Review* article, Jack Mitchell,

---

30 PwC is the brand name for PriceWaterhouseCoopers Int. Ltd.
31 PwC Family Business Survey 2021. "From Trust to Impact: Why Family Businesses Need to Act Now to Ensure Their Legacies Tomorrow." https://bit.ly/TrustToImpact

author and chairman of Mitchell Stores, a third-generation clothing retailer, shared his philosophy on hiring family.[32]

Mitchell's philosophy can be summarized by these two rules: (1) After graduating from college or the equivalent, you must work elsewhere for at least five years before you can join the family business, and (2) you must be a good fit for an actual job at the company.

The first few years of a career are critical to creating self-awareness, confidence, and a sense of independence, but all too often, individuals are stripped of this experience from pressure or expectations of an immediate job in the family company.

The same failure-recovery-success cycle discussed earlier in this chapter may need to be repeated in the early years of a career. Welcome the challenge with realistic emotional support that doesn't involve the safety net of a job at the family company.

Inheriting financial wealth with perspective and a sense of personal identity can be challenging, but it is critical to a successful intergenerational transfer. As detailed earlier, communication and intentional sharing of stories and perspective are incumbent on parents to share with their heirs.

Consider the creation of beneficiaries who have a sense of independence. Also consider that the transfer of culture, priorities, and lessons is as big a priority as transferring wealth.

Big dividends come from families that spend as much time on the softer, personal character-building priorities and non-financial inheritance topics as they spend on tax planning, legal structuring, and investment management decisions.

---

32 Jack Mitchell. 2020. *How to Decide Who Can Join the Family Business.* Harvard Business School.

Career Crossroads

After college, I remember the overwhelming feeling of not knowing where I fit in the world. I was doing my best to find a good job—one that would allow me financial independence. There wasn't much more to my criteria. If I could afford an apartment and a car—and, as soon as possible, and an engagement ring so I could propose to Jill—life would be good.

When I started working at Valley Forge and interacted with clients, it made me even more driven to do well. But among my first clients, I was especially envious of Claudia Wickham for the fact that she had a place in a successful landscaping and snow removal business of which her dad was one of two partners.

The business was the largest of its kind in the Boston area. And as the oldest of three children, Claudia had a reserved spot she was expected to fill after college.

How lucky she was! Or so I thought.

During my initial interview to help her create a financial plan, Claudia told me how she won the science fair every year in high school. She thrived in the classroom and went on to study chemistry at the University of Michigan. It was clear Claudia had a passion for the elements.

"The more beakers and bubbles in my life, the happier I was in college," she told me.

Claudia also had found love in Rich, the two having married shortly before our meeting. They were a perfect match—the type of couple you would cast in a movie. He was as handsome as she was beautiful.

A couple of years after I first met Claudia and Rich, I visited them in the Boston suburbs. They were expecting their first child, a girl. I could relate as Jill had a similar due date, also with our first. The couple had already bought a house, and Claudia shared that her parents were going to set up a 529 college saving plan for their new granddaughter.

Could they have been any more fortunate?

At the time, Jill and I were living in an apartment, and we were proud of our modest early career accomplishments, but I felt so behind in the game of life. We barely had enough to put a down payment on a home, let alone start thinking about college savings!

Fast forward 10 years. By this time, our families were getting together about every year as I traveled to meet with Claudia and Rich. Our family and theirs had a lot in common—both were busy raising three young children.

But Claudia had changed. She had gained a lot of weight and was drinking excessively. In fact, during our visits, there was rarely a moment Claudia didn't have a drink in her hand. She was no longer the picture of pure joy. Quite the opposite.

When I asked how work was going, Claudia had some choice words to describe her dad and the business. This was *very* different from her response in the past.

Claudia shared that she and her dad weren't on speaking terms. He and his business partner were arguing over the future equity split of the business, and the work environment had become toxic. Claudia was working a lot of hours. She was miserable.

She told me that the fighting had been going on for a long time, and that she felt stuck. But she was loyal to her family and to the family business. Maybe too loyal.

Claudia and Rich were considering leaving Massachusetts. But not long after, I got news that Claudia and her siblings had started a competing company in Boston. They had the reluctant support of their father since he was still fighting with his business partner.

But the new company struggled. The siblings were incapable of running the business well and were blaming each other for its demise. Their company had the same dysfunctional culture as their dad's company. They didn't have a business plan, and roles weren't clearly defined.

Without a plan, without specific roles or job descriptions, the company was set up to fail.

As the firstborn, Claudia felt responsible for the company's success and took on too many projects. She also took on the role of peacemaker—and trying to break up fights between her brother and sister soon felt like a part-time job.

Her brother was good at estimating projects but had a horrible work ethic. He rarely worked more than six hours a day. Her sister was good at math but never had training as an accountant. She was expected to keep the books, but cash was always short.

I believe the outcome could have been different if the Wickhams had been given formal training while they were working at the family business. Instead, due to the constant conflict and infighting, they were left on their own to develop work habits.

Rather than being a fresh start, the new landscaping and snow removal startup completely backfired. Claudia worked seven days a week trying to hold everything together. Her long days followed by nightly drinking were unsustainable. Her home life suffered. Rich was unhappy. Everyone was unhappy.

After two years of trying to make things work, the company closed their doors. But not before Claudia collapsed in her office and almost died. She was just 49.

Two months after Claudia was released from the hospital, she told Rich she wanted a divorce. Despite her husband pleading to seek therapy and create change together, he became the target of all the years of struggle.

Claudia wanted a complete change of everything in her life, and that included their marriage of 23 years.

It turned out that joining the family business was a curse, not a blessing.

Looking back, I can't help but wonder what the outcome might have been had Claudia become a chemist. It was clearly her passion, and she was good at it.

Claudia will eventually inherit substantial wealth—enough to retire very comfortably. Financially, she'll be OK. But in every other aspect of her life, Claudia is lacking, in part because she has missed out on the lessons that come from the principles outlined in this book—particularly, nurturing independence.

In *A Wealth of Possibilities*, Ellen Miley Perry writes, "To flourish, the family must nurture and grow human capital with the same passion the original wealth creator put toward building financial capital."[33]

I agree wholeheartedly.

Counselor's Insights

Claudia's father was not interviewed for this book. We don't know what his motivations were for creating a job and paving a career path at his company for Claudia. We can assume he thought it would make his daughter's life easier. Maybe he thought it would guarantee her financial stability and success or avoid any unnecessary struggle or suffering on her part.

Creating separate, independent human beings is no small task. Thankfully, there are many great books and resources on parenting. For a curated list, visit www.TheGreatestGiftBook.com.

---

33 Eileen Miley Perry. 2012. *A Wealth of Possibilities: Navigating Family, Money, and Legacy*. Egremont Press.

Here, I'd like to simply suggest a mantra of sorts that can be applied across many scenarios, though gently and with subtlety: *As a parent, you need to be OK with your kids* not *being OK.*

Why on earth would I suggest you be OK with your kids suffering?

Let me start by being *super* clear: It doesn't mean you shouldn't care. It doesn't mean you shouldn't empathize with their pain. Nor does it mean you should ignore them, pacify them, or provide platitudes to their not being OK.

So, what does it mean? Be with them, support them, and listen to them, but do not try to fix them or their pain.

Trust me, if it worked and was possible, I would do it too. I'd want to fix all the challenges my kids encounter. But we can't. When we try to, we deny our children our authentic comfort and the incredible learning experience that comes with adversity and pain.

Of course, there are times when the pain is just too much to bear. That is a crisis—and different rules apply. That's not what I'm talking about here, though. I'm not referring to crisis situations when I say, "I'm OK with my kids being *not OK.*"

When we don't allow our kids to experience, express, and process struggles and suffering, we set them up for transmitting the pain elsewhere, even internalizing it.

Children need full permission to *not* be OK at times. They need permission to fail, to feel sad, frustrated, and overwhelmed, and they need permission *to express* that they don't feel OK.

If they get the sense—implied or said directly—that it makes us uncomfortable that they are in pain, they will shove it down and repress and hide it.

One way to conceptualize depression is to see it as *hard emotions*—hurt, pain or anger—*turned inward*. When we or our children are not given the freedom to express, process, or adapt to these emotions, they become internalized.

Of course, we can't keep this from ever happening to our children, but we can contribute to it by making it unwelcoming for them to express hard emotions.

This is a difficult concept to explain and even harder to enact as parent.

Here is a suggestion: picture someone you would go to when you face a struggle, maybe an old friend or a family member who you know is safe to be vulnerable with. Why did you pick that person in particular?

- Does that person seem calm? Are they generally stable to lean on?
- Do they have the internal resources and energy to listen well and let you express the distressing emotions you have surrounding the struggle you're facing?
- Do you get the sense that your struggle causes them extreme stress—or that they can hold this with you while maintaining their individual sense of regulation?
- Do they convey sincere empathy and care and willingness to support you while also freeing you of any worry that you've severely agitated them by sharing your vulnerable state?

As parents, providing this type of support is our goal. But it's not easy. It takes work on our own emotions. Sayings like "You can't fill from an empty cup," or "Build your home on a foundation of rock instead of sand" certainly apply here.

We need to keep our emotional state full and solid to support our children where they are.

Be aware of your state of regulation and stay grounded so your kids know you are solid, separate, and able to hold firm—even when they experience pain. This is especially true when it comes to failure. It gives them that freedom to take risks, fail, and formulate their own sense of self.

As best you can, be OK even when *they* are not OK.

Tangible Tools for Nurturing Independence

- **Start early**. Being alright when your seven-year-old is distraught by being left out of the recess kickball game is a much easier place to practice these principles than when your 17-year-old is rejected by their first-choice college. When stakes feel higher, it is harder to empathize without trying to fix things.
- **Never be more excited—or more distraught—than your kids about an accomplishment or failure than they are**. A child hits a home run in baseball, but the mom's the one that can't stop talking about it. Or a child misses a big competitive cut, and the dad is the one that can't shake the bad mood or is more determined than the child to get it next time. Let your kids set the tone and tell you how they want to celebrate or be consoled. The success or failure is theirs. Lead with curiosity. Ask how they would like to celebrate or how they can be supported.
- **Regulate yourself.** Build your foundation. Fill your cup. Grieve how their losses impact you separately from them. Work intentionally on your being alright with the outcome.

In Short | Striving to create self-sufficient heirs is critical to a peaceful intergenerational transfer of wealth. Giving your heirs the space, opportunity, and support to do things on their own, along with giving them the permission to fail helps them move from enmeshment to independence.

It may seem counterintuitive, but one of the most useful tools to prepare inheritors for receiving assets is to encourage giving. That is the topic of the next chapter.

7

Encourage Giving

To ease another's heartache is to forget one's own.
~Abraham Lincoln

What makes us feel entitled to an inheritance? When I've asked individuals of all ages and wealth levels about expectations around a future inheritance, it is rare to have someone say, "I hope I get nothing. I'm not planning on inheriting anything, nor do I want anything."

It is more common to hear specific estimates or assumptions of assets and amounts to be received at the death of parents. When I probe deeper and ask how they know about the amount they will inherit, interviewees will share clues they've picked up on. They've been playing detective, trying

Principle 7:
Encourage Giving
Destructive Emotion:
Greed
Constructive Emotion:
Generosity
Proposition:
Charity is pure love.

to estimate an amount based on limited information and snippets of conversations.

Very few people know exactly how much they will inherit. Communication from their parents is rarely clear, so they have to make assumptions which lead to expectations. And expectations can lead to a feeling of entitlement.

Of those I've interviewed, the few who have given the rare answer that they don't feel entitled to an inheritance—or they simply don't want or need it—are best equipped to receive one.

When we start counting an anticipated inheritance among our assets, we set ourselves up for disappointment and conflict.

Avoiding a Christmas Letdown

The days, weeks, and months leading up to December 25th can be rich with the idyllic images of snowy cabins in the woods, stockings hung by the chimney, favorite holiday songs, hot cocoa by a warm fire . . . and presents!

Children are encouraged to send a wish list to Santa, young adults are asked to make a list for their mom and dad, and even adults are solicited for things they need or what they wouldn't buy for themselves. Gift givers try to find ways to surprise their loved ones with the perfect gift.

Christmas morning is always full of anticipation. Culturally, we are urged to show surprise and excitement when opening our present, even if we are really thinking, *Oh no . . . more socks I will never wear.*

Indeed, it doesn't take long for the letdown to set in. And a Christmas letdown is best illustrated when a child asks, "That's it?" or bluntly states, "This isn't what I asked for."

With time and maturity, kids (hopefully) learn the polite way to receive gifts even when they're a bit disappointed. Best of all is if they truly are grateful for the presents they receive.

An inheritance is likely the biggest gift any of us will ever receive in our lifetime. But if it's a surprise, like a Christmas gift, it will possibly come with some level of disappointment.

Maybe the inheritance isn't as large as you thought or not the way you wanted it. You may have to share it with others, or the assets are hard to manage or sell.

My observation is that most people overestimate what they stand to inherit, and they underestimate the effect taxes will have on their newfound wealth.

Avoid the Christmas letdown effect by creating an awareness of how your estate plan is structured. Also, specify who will get what and when they'll get it. (More about that in Chapter 9.)

||||||||||||

On a ride to the airport one day, I was talking to my ride-share driver about college, our kids, and the cost of college. He commented that colleges are aggressive about asking for donations, starting even before a child graduates.

His daughter's college had recently announced a $13.5 million donation by a woman through her will, he told me, adding, "Her kids must have been so pissed!" This is not an unusual perspective. But who knows how the donor's kids felt? They likely had a family connection to the school. Maybe they were all fully supportive of the donation.

I certainly hope the gift was well thought out and communicated as part of an estate plan. Call me an optimist, but I like to imagine the donation allowed the family to celebrate their mom, grandma—maybe great-grandma—with a ceremony in her honor.

My driver's comment caused me to wonder how I'd feel if my parents donated some of their hard-earned savings when they die.

Granted, I'd feel jealous if they left it to someone else, but maybe less jealous if it went to a charitable organization. I'm pretty sure I'd be upset if it were a charity I didn't like.

It's funny that, somehow, I feel some ownership of my parents' estate and would want to control even a gift to charity. I may have an opinion, but should I have a say in their final wishes?

What Keeps Families Together

In their book *Entrusted*, authors David R. York and Andrew L. Howell make a wonderful observation of what holds families together.

> We tend to think of families in a vertical fashion, like the family tree, starting with mom and dad and then moving downward to kids and grandkids. In our experience, families are really more of a hub and spoke. Mom and dad are in the middle, the common connection point, with the kids radiating out like spokes . . . As soon as mom and dad are gone, however, the connection point goes away, and the kids drift off in their own directions.[34]

---

34   David R. York & Andrew L. Howell. 2015. *Entrusted: Building a Legacy That Lasts.* YH Publishing, LLC.

As an antidote to drifting apart, York and Howell suggest replacing mom, dad, and their money as the connecting hub with something else.

Promoting humility (as suggested in Chapter 5), and encouraging giving are ways to keep the next generations in communion and at peace with each other by providing a common connection—that central hub.

Charity is a tremendous tool. It is hard to be charitable and gracious while also feeling greedy. What's more, there's evidence showing that giving to charity is as beneficial to the donor as it is to the recipient.

Centering the family culture around acts of charity and supporting those who have needs we can help meet can create a strong bond among generations. Charity can also help family members who struggle with entitlement—helping them refocus on the needs of others rather than on themselves.

For me, giving is often easier to think about than to practice.

No matter the amount you give or the time that you donate, charity takes work and repetition. So, as you would with anything important, be deliberate with your gifts to charity. Set clear goals and objectives for giving, then create a plan and execute it.

As a family, be honest about your expectations. Do you only require a tax receipt for your giving? Or do you hope to be involved in the work of the charity you're giving to?

Many parents are surprised at the initial lack of engagement from their children when it comes to charitable giving. This is not surprising. Like anything, it takes practice and reinforcement. For those who involve their family and invite them to choose which charities to donate to, children and adult beneficiaries are often non-responsive to the first few attempts. This is a good sign! They understand the value of a dollar. And choosing *one* charity among all the choices available is hard.

Your heirs need consistent leadership and guidance. If it is important to you, make charitable giving a regular conversation, a part of your family culture. If you need help, find a charitable consultant. We list charitable consulting resources and reviews on our website, www.TheGreatestGiftBook.com.

In their whitepaper, "Feeling Good about Giving: The Benefits (and Costs) of Self-Interested Charitable Behavior," the authors tested whether giving leads to increased happiness.[35] They cite scientific studies, prior published studies, and their own random field study, concluding: "As predicted, participants asked to spend their windfall in a pro-social fashion were happier at the end of the day than were the participants in the personal spending condition."

||||||||||||

What holds your family together? Will it still be there when you are gone? Charity is a common bind, but not the only one. If you are charitably inclined, share it with your children and heirs.

Share your story and why certain charities are important to you. Even if they don't understand at first or if they are not at a stage in life when they can appreciate it fully, your charitable involvement will become part of your legacy—and the glue that helps hold your family together.

---

[35] Lalin Anik, Lara B. Aknin, Michael I. Norton, Elizabeth W. Dunn. 2009. *Feeling Good about Giving: The Benefits (and Costs) of Self-Interested Charitable Behavior.* Harvard Business School.

Service Trips and Service Tourism

Many high schools and colleges offer the opportunity to travel for service trips during school breaks. Some of these options are in the US, while many are for international volunteer trips.

Having seen firsthand the life-changing impact such an opportunity had on my children, I highly recommend that you encourage and incentivize your children or grandchildren to seek out such opportunities.

Our children each had the opportunity to travel internationally for between 10 days and two weeks. One served at an orphanage in Armenia, another helped dig a water line in the Dominican Republic, and the third helped with beach cleanup, painting, and a landscape refresh of a library in Costa Rica.

The trips combined service with relaxation and tours. The combination of service and the adventure of travel was exciting. Better yet, the hands-on perspective of serving alongside and spending time among those with access to fewer resources—even learning from them—cannot be preached or taught in the classroom.

One of our sons broke down crying when he got home from his service trip realizing the garage where we keep our cars was larger than the average family dwelling where he had just served. It gave him a deep appreciation for things we take for granted: running water, electricity, and a sturdy, spacious home.

As a result of our children's positive service trip experiences, our family has sought out service opportunities during several of our vacations. On a trip to the Florida panhandle, we helped with storm cleanup from Hurricane Michael. During a visit to South Africa, we spent a day helping prepare a community garden for spring planting.

In each case, we interacted with the people we were serving and enjoyed our leisure activities with a positive boost to perspective and gratitude for the gift of travel and relaxation.

||||||||||||

The Cleveland Clinic makes the case that giving makes you feel happier, something they refer to as a helper's high. They summarize numerous studies stating there is evidence that, "during gift-giving behaviors, humans secrete 'feel-good' chemicals in our brains, such as serotonin (a mood-mediating chemical), dopamine (a feel-good chemical) and oxytocin (a compassion and bonding chemical)."[36]

Similar to our family's service trips, you can find ample opportunities to volunteer wherever you go. Research ahead of time.

Many charitable organizations provide preplanned activities for those interested in service tourism, sometimes called "voluntourism." But this concept has received its share of criticism as the free foreign labor, however transformative it might be for us as visitors, often robs locals of the chance to earn much-needed money on, say, a construction project.

Professor Nancy Gard McGehee at Virginia Tech has conducted more than 25 years of research on this topic and would like to see voluntourism recast as "transformative tourism." She and her colleagues suggest visitors would be rewarded by gaining a better understanding of people's lives and the way the economics of charity work.

By all means, visit people who need help, McGehee says. "But do it beside me and hear who I am. Get to know me and not all

---

36 "Why Giving Is Good for Your Health." *Cleveland Clinic Health Essentials.* December 2022.

those stereotypes about me. And then go home and see if there's something you're doing that somehow perpetuates my situation."[37]

In a series of *National Geographic* articles, Kenn Budd offers this guidance before embarking on a volunteer trip: Research various organizations. Speak with previous volunteers. Ask questions. Do local people run the organization? Is it creating dependency? How does the community benefit? Does the work match your skills?[38, 39]

As with anything important, be intentional about the purpose of your trip and how you can best help.

One of my favorite estate attorneys, one who works with several of our clients, captures the spirit of giving time and giving money with this quote, "Give with warm hands, not cold." In other words, give while you are alive—don't wait until you are dead. This applies to charitable giving as well as lifetime gifts to beneficiaries and trusts.

Giving to charity during your lifetime provides your family the opportunity to bond, educates your inheritors, plus it benefits those in need in the current moment. So, challenge yourself to give consistent smaller amounts *now* versus a larger lump sum later, foregoing the recognition and naming rights a larger "splash" gift would bring.

Charities need the money now. The return on your investment can be measured by the current use of the funds, not how the money would grow in an investment portfolio.

Charity is the antidote for feelings of entitlement. And charity done intentionally and freely reinforces gratitude. Consequently,

---

37 Tina Rosenberg. "The Business of Voluntourism: Do Western Do-gooders Actually Do Harm?" *The Guardian*. September 13, 2018.
38 Ken Budd. "Five Myths About Voluntourism." *National Geographic*. November 9, 2018.
39 Ken Budd. "Does Voluntourism Help? Here Are the Questions to Ask Before You Go." *National Geographic*. June 27, 2019.

gratitude naturally diminishes feelings of entitlement as the sense of thankfulness for what *is* becomes more important than what one *has*.

The Gift of Giving

I'm sure you've heard the saying, "Give with your three Ts: time, talent, and treasure." Still, when it comes to giving, most folks think of simply giving money.

But there are countless opportunities in the US to volunteer through service, whether giving of your time—say, at a soup kitchen, at a local school, or at a non-profit such as your library or an animal shelter—or giving of your talent, which is usually more specialized. This is about donating what you're really good at doing, helping an organization or individual without getting paid. One example would be to serve on the board of a 501(c)(3) charity.

My friend Chris is a great example of giving his time through service.

Chris and I enjoy running with our dogs once or twice a week, often at the crack of dawn. By the end of our run, it sometimes feels like we've solved all the world's problems. He thinks we should start a podcast with all the big revelations that come to us while we run, but I think he's nuts.

Like me, Chris grew up Catholic, but our expression of faith is different. For as long as I've known Chris, he's been volunteering at a nearby shelter. On one of our runs, Chris told me, "Going to the soup kitchen is way better than going to Sunday mass."

So, I decided to join him at a soup kitchen one morning, and the experience left me thoroughly impressed. The soup kitchen where Chris serves is run by the Missionaries of Charity, a worldwide religious community founded by Mother Teresa (now Saint Teresa of Calcutta).

This order runs a shelter not far from our town. It's a haven for battered women, and they serve daily meals to anyone who shows up. Most of the guests are homeless and hungry.

Volunteering at the shelter starts with unpacking and organizing the ingredients. The sisters in charge organize the volunteers and gently guide the food preparation and the setting of the tables. They have a plan, and they are highly efficient.

By the time people start showing up for meals, the place smells amazing. The aroma wafts through the halls, welcoming hungry guests.

Once everyone is seated, the sisters lead in prayer. The hungriest of hungry patiently wait, the smell of a warm meal in the air, while some guests participate in prayer.

For me, taking time to reflect on gratitude and praising God made the meal taste even better, and I imagine the experience being the same for many of the guests.

After my first morning of service, I agreed with Chris. Serving at the soup kitchen is a spiritual, uplifting experience!

The Moores and Their Scholarship Fund

Jim and Betsy Moore are both former high-school teachers and arguably some of the nicest people I have ever met.

Our meetings are always at their home, and I always knew I would be welcomed with the perfect cup of coffee and a slice of freshly baked cake or some sweet pastry. Hospitality is one of their top values.

Jim had taught math and Betsy chemistry. And while teaching in the public school system wasn't the type of career known to set you up for lifelong financial security, the couple had done well saving and making careful investment decisions throughout their life. With their two children grown, self-sufficient, and having families of their own, Jim and Betsy are comfortably retired.

Even after purchasing a vacation home on the Gulf Coast, the Moores still had a $4.5 million investment portfolio. Income from their investments combined with their monthly pension benefits was more than enough to support their income needs.

But they knew their reality didn't match that of many families in their community, especially at the school where they had taught until retirement. That school was in a rural county and had a lower-than-average college attendance rate among its students.

Jim and Betsy wanted to start a scholarship fund. First, they knew they needed to speak with their children.

When their family gathered at their beach house for Thanksgiving one year, Jim and Betsy shared the idea of the Moore Family Scholarship Fund with their children and their spouses. All of them had benefited from having a solid college education, and knowing how dedicated Jim and Betsy were to education, the kids were highly supportive of the idea.

They all agreed to offer a scholarship each year to one student who couldn't afford college themselves. But knowing that there are other scholarships available for those who did well academically, Jim and Betsy wanted their funds to go to a student with C+ or better, someone in the "middle of the pack," so to speak.

Now, several years in, the scholarship has grown to four students every year.

In the first year of college, the scholarship is $2,500. The next year, it's $5,000. The $2,500 increase per year also goes for the third and fourth years.

That means if a student stays in college and continues to do well, they will have received $25,000 in scholarship funding from the Moore Family Scholarship Fund! Meanwhile, nothing keeps them from applying for financial aid or for other scholarships.

Jim and Betsy review each application and personally interview each student, but a school administrator has the final say as to who gets that year's scholarships. The couple meets with all the recipients once a year. (Naturally, they always bring pastries to those meetings.)

So far, 13 students who may not have considered tertiary education have graduated college thanks to the Moores. And many of those keep in touch with the Moore family. Of all the recipients, only *one* dropped out of college.

Currently, the Moores pay out $100,000 in scholarship fees every year—a tax-deductible donation, seeing that it is done in cooperation with the school district. Their gift is a little more than 2% of their investment portfolio per year—typically less than the annual growth of the portfolio.

Through it all, the couple has had the full support of and involvement from their children. Jim and Betsy Moore have created a valuable cultural tradition within their family. They have also modeled to the student-beneficiaries what true hospitality looks like.

Creating an Engaged Second Generation

Rob and Bev Wright sold their family farm in 2016. They told me deciding to sell the farm was possibly the hardest decision they ever made. Situated in an idyllic setting in Lancaster County, just west of our office, they found themselves at the planned intersection of two major interstate highways. The value of their land skyrocketed. It made no logical sense to continue farming on this property.

Years prior, when my children were toddlers, the Wrights hosted us for a campout. We brought our tents and sleeping bags, roasted hot dogs over an open fire, and in the morning after being woken up by the roosters, we swung from the tire swing into the farm pond.

Even today, when my family talks about fun adventures we've had, that trip comes up as a cherished family memory, so I can imagine how hard it was for Rob and Bev to sell the farm and all the memories it had associated with it.

After taxes, the Wrights received $30 million for their property. It was more money than they ever dreamed they would have as a family. After careful consideration and much deliberation with their estate lawyer, accountant, and me, they decided to donate $5 million to create the Wright Family Foundation.

The foundation has a very broad mandate: It exists to support any public charity in the United States.

Since the inception in 2016, their children—Bud, Eve, and Shane, ranging from their early to late twenties at the time—were named as the foundation's officers, the ones who would decide who would receive annual grants. The parents committed not to exercise any influence on the kids' decision.

Bud, Eve, and Shane have taken their roles very seriously. They meet semiannually to review the investment performance and plan for the gifts they will make. Rob and Bev are extremely pleased with how it has become a common purpose for their children.

In 2016, they made small gifts to recognizable charities. Looking back, it made a lot of sense. Without the experience of operating the foundation and the time to research charities, this approach allowed them to get started.

In 2017, Hurricane Harvey hit Houston and became a focal point for the foundation's efforts. Half of the grants that year went to charities that were serving victims.

Since that time, they have all taken a keen interest in how they can best use the foundation to help those in need.

Rob and Bev have been so impressed with the way the foundation has impacted their family and the relationships with their children and their spouses, they gave another $1.5 million to the foundation in 2022.

When I shared with the Wrights that I was writing this book and wanted to include their story, they commented on how their family foundation reinforces several of the very important principles we have discussed so far, especially developing a common purpose, defining roles, and encouraging giving.

||||||||||||

Charity in any form, practiced regularly as a part of the family culture, helps prevent feelings of entitlement. Family members who give their time, talent, and treasure are focused outward—on how they can help others—not simply inward, on themselves.

Encourage giving to reinforce generosity and mindfulness to leaving the world a better place than you found it.

Thoughts on Charity

When Helping Hurts: How to Alleviate Poverty Without Hurting the Poor . . . and Yourself by Steve Corbett and Brian Fikkert is written from a Christian perspective.[40] Their emphasis on conversion to

---

40   Steve Corbett & Brian Fikkert. 2012. *When Helping Hurts: How to Alleviate Poverty without Hurting the Poor . . . and Yourself.* Moody Publishers.

Christianity may be off-putting to some, but I found several parts of the book helpful. These concepts may also be helpful to you and your family when discussing and planning the best plan for giving.

Corbett and Fikkert distinguish between three types of needs: relief, rehabilitation, and development.

- Relief is the urgent and temporary provision of emergency aid to reduce immediate suffering.
- Rehabilitation is the shift from working for emergency victims to working with them to restore people and their communities to the positive elements of their pre-crisis conditions.
- Development is the ongoing change that moves all people, the "helpers" and the "helped."

The authors emphasize that charitable activities must identify which category of need to address in order to avoid misguided giving. And they assert that the biggest mistake "is applying relief in situations in which rehabilitation or development is the appropriate intervention."[41]

These insights along with other themes from the book have caused Jill and I to be more thoughtful and deliberate about our charitable giving. We also started a conversation about charity with our children.

Part of that discussion is the commitment Jill and I have made to donate all the profits from book sales to support mental healthcare.

Jill is involved with the Peacemaker Center, a non-profit counseling service in Pennsylvania. Part of Peacemaker's mission is to provide free or reduced-rate services for the clients who need it.

---

[41] Corbett & Fikkert, *When Helping Hurts.*

Jill's involvement with Peacemaker has provided our family insight into the importance of access to counseling, including for those who cannot afford to pay the hourly rate.

As a family, we decided that we'll donate to public charities—like Peacemaker—that we find to be doing the best work for those in need of mental health support. We will be careful to consider whether the needs being met are relief, rehabilitative, or developmental.

The Benefits of Creating a Private Foundation

Private foundations were discussed in Chapter 1 as a tool for some families to develop a common purpose while doing good. Private foundations are considered charities, and similar income tax deductions apply to gifts made to one.

In any given year, the law requires private foundations to donate a minimum of 5% of assets. However, I recommend donating 10–15% to avoid an unhealthy focus on the principal sum instead of the real goal, which is to *make contributions to other public charities*.

Setting up a private foundation is straightforward and can be accomplished with the help of a qualified attorney. Foundations can also take the form of a trust (which requires having one or more trustees) or a corporation (which requires a board of directors and officers).

For high-net-worth families, creating a private foundation under the terms of their will is a tax-efficient option. However, waiting to create such a foundation until the passing of the parents doesn't encourage gifting and the benefits discussed in this chapter.

Waiting until death to establish a private foundation robs the children—those likely tasked with the management of the foundation—of the guidance and practice while you as parents are still around.

You'll need to devote both time and intentionality to set up a foundation that serves your desires as its creators. Before creating a private foundation, you'll need to establish a vision and mission, governance, and reporting. You'll also need to hire staff and appoint the governance team—directors, trustees, and officers.

Depending on the size and complexity of the foundation, staffing can be done directly or through outsourcing. Many foundations start by sharing the accounting, investment management, and legal professionals of the foundation creator. Over time, staffing needs will change and those responsible for governance will determine how to best staff the foundation.

Again, we'll discuss communication and family governance in greater depth in Chapter 9. Here, suffice it to say that properly formed vision and mission statements along with having clear strategic plans are paramount to the successful launch and maintenance of a private foundation.[42]

The **vision statement** captures an overarching theme that can be used to motivate and direct the efforts of everyone involved. It should include the overarching goal of the foundation.

The **mission statement** provides an opportunity to provide strategic guidance and bring everyone involved together around a common goal or set of goals.

The **strategic plan** of the foundation outlines the annual giving amount and the time frame for the assets to be given to charity.

Building a governance team for your private foundation is also important. Such a team will ensure your wishes are carried out.

As with any organization, practice and repetition will create the culture of your private foundation. This cannot be emphasized

---

[42] It's worth noting that private foundations cannot raise funds from the public. That would be considered a public foundation, which requires additional setup and annual compliance.

enough. Foundations take time and effort to create a cadence, prioritize needs, and satisfy the desires of its creators.

Set up quarterly meetings to initiate, instill, and reinforce the vision and mission. Be decisive and replace non-participating members from the governance team. If your intent is to disperse the foundation assets within a certain number of years, let it be known.

Reporting includes the performance of the invested foundation portfolio, the impact the foundation is making to specific charities and causes, and the monitoring and systematic grading of grant recipients.

- Review performance of the portfolio quarterly. Professionals need to be held accountable to benchmarking and fee efficiency.
- Know that it can be a challenge to measure impact. It is more complicated than making a list of which charities or non-profits received support. Impact measurements include where and how the funding was used.

You can monitor grant recipients by using resources such as GuideStar and Charity Navigator, but monitoring should also include presentations by representatives of charities you support along with interviews with those responsible for the stewardship of funds.

Counselor's Insights

This chapter centers on creating an environment of contentment surrounding an inheritance. It's about avoiding a reaction that resembles the comment from Sean's ride-share driver, that a major donor's kids would be miffed at her generous donation to a university.

Instead, what if there was a behavioral formula to induce contentment? Well, there is. It's not foolproof, but it offers some insights that can give you a place from which to start.

In *Hacking of the American Mind,* author Robert H. Lustig explores America's struggle with depression and addiction.[43] Lustig is a neuroscientist, and he suggests that we can increase or decrease the production of serotonin and dopamine to influence our mood state and increase our ability to cope with stress.

As you may know, serotonin is the contentment chemical. It gives the sensation of *this feels good,* and *I need nothing more; I am content.* Its effects are long lasting and ethereal, *of the spirit.* Anti-depressants are usually made to sustain serotonin levels in the brain.

Dopamine is the pleasure chemical. It helps to motivate us. Dopamine gives the sensation that *I like it* and *I want more of it.* It is short lived and visceral, *of the body.* Eating food, having sex, winning a game, or earning money are examples of experiences that lead to the release of dopamine.

Emotional balance and survival require that our brain releases both of these chemicals. Thanks to amazing advances in brain imaging, we can now prove what was only theoretical in the past:

---

43 Robert H. Lustig. 2018. *Hacking of the American Mind: The Science Behind the Corporate Takeover of Our Bodies and Brains.* Avery.

that certain activities and food choices increase or decrease serotonin and dopamine.

Specifically, connecting, coping, cooking, and contributing have been proven to increase serotonin in the brain, thus leading to a greater experience of contentment. Lustig calls these the four Cs.

Below is a reflection on the first and last C in this list—connecting and contributing. Connect with the members of your family and determine to contribute to the world. Using these principles of brain science intentionally will bring an air of contentment and satisfaction to your estate-planning and inheritance experience.

Tangible Tools for Creating Contentment

- **Connect face to face.** This causes your brain to release serotonin. In the context of this book, examples of such connections include bonding over family dinner, vacations, or holiday traditions. Likewise, participating in acts of service with others in your family will also provide a sense of connecting. It will leave you feeling good, that you are content.
- **Contribute to something beyond yourself.** This also produces serotonin and includes being charitable in any form, whether monetarily, giving of your time, or even being charitable with your assumptions! What a motivator for assuming the best intentions of others in your family—not only for the sake of your relationship but also for the benefit of your mood state.

|||||||||||||

In Short | Giving of your time, talents, and assets alongside your beneficiaries helps model and demonstrate love and teaches generosity. It also becomes an antidote to greed.

Next, we'll discuss the importance of inclusion for all members of the family, including spouses and other new additions to the family, by creating a safe environment—one that reinforces being enough, feeling safe, and instilling confidence in generations to follow.

8
Create a Safe Environment

The moment you see how important it is to love yourself, you will stop making others suffer.
~Buddha

People can be puzzling. Interacting with some may be easy; they're comfortable to be around. Getting to that same comfort with others may take years. This is no different within families.

Comfortable interactions often depend on each person's sense of security—whether they feel safe and connected. Safety in this sense is rooted in contentment, in self-confidence from accomplishments, a meaningful life, or simply being enough.

Generally, people who feel content are easier to be around. They evoke a sense of safety.

Principle 8:
Create a Safe Environment
Destructive Emotion:
Insecurity
Constructive Emotion:
Confidence
Proposition:
Trust creates safety.

Receiving an inheritance comes at a time of great change. For some, this type of change or transition causes immense internal conflict. You can avoid that conflict spilling over into family interactions by fostering a sense of safety. And feeling safe, in turn, offers a sense of comfort, even confidence.

One way you can nurture such a sense of confidence is by reinforcing family ties and sharing information.

We tend to spend our lives saving money, protecting our assets, and planning for retirement. But we spend nowhere near enough time communicating our wishes and dealing with the emotional aspects of inheritance and wealth.

Sharing your wishes will provide a sense of comfort with your heirs. It will also lower anxiety and insecurity during times of change—times fraught with conflict.

Similarly, speaking about your pride in each person's accomplishments and reiterating that they are enough and cherished for who they are as individuals provide a solid foundation of confidence.

Neglecting to trust your heirs with your wishes and thoughts does the opposite. It can open the door to immense discontent and erode a sense of safety, leading to a feeling of insecurity. This can cause an implosion within your family.

This certainly was the case with the Green family from Charleston, South Carolina.

Four Siblings, Two Points of View

When Patrick Green died, his entire estate worth more than $20 million was set aside in a spousal trust. Jane, his wife of more than 40 years, was entitled to the trust income. She was also able to receive additional distributions of principal if she needed it for health, education, maintenance, or support. This is very common and in estate planning, it's referred to as the HEMS standard.

The annual income generated by the trust was much more than Jane could spend in a year, so the trust kept growing and growing for the eventual benefit of Steve and Jane's four children and nine grandchildren.

A couple of years after Patrick died, I visited Jane at her South Carolina home. We had plans to go for dinner at a local fish fry. Jane shared how excited she was for me to meet her new friend, David, also a widower and a father to one adult son. The two of them had met through mutual friends from their church, and they shared many of the same interests.

I could immediately see why Jane was so excited for me to meet David. He was a true gentleman! As for Jane, it was the first time since Patrick's passing that I saw her smile and truly enjoy herself.

She had found a true companion and had a renewed outlook on life. It seemed to me a wonderful, mutually beneficial relationship. I enjoyed hearing about their plans for an upcoming trip to Europe.

I had hardly returned to Pennsylvania when I got a call from Jane's oldest son, Tom. Clearly distraught, Tom asked if I had met David and what my impression of him was.

Of course, I told him how happy I was for Jane to have found someone with similar interests, including travel, and how nice it must be to have a companion after the pain of losing her husband.

To my surprise, Tom launched into a stream of affronts. He called David a money grabber and a leech. He said that he and his sister, Michelle, were convinced David was only dating Jane for her money, that he was taking advantage of Jane's good nature.

Not once did I have that impression. Instead, it was evident to me that Tom and Michelle were concerned about their inheritance—more than they were concerned about their mom's wellbeing. Tom was exhibiting suspicion, jealousy, and greed.

There was a stark contrast between the harmony Jane found and the jealousy and discontent it created for two of her children. There was something about seeing their mom with a new person that really upset them. They were what can be described as detractors.

Naturally, seeing a parent date again after losing their spouse is hard for any child. What wasn't normal was their level of rage and suspicion. They treated David poorly and found reasons to be upset with his involvement with their mother.

I knew all four of Jane's children, so I wasn't surprised when John called soon after getting news of his brother's call to me. He assured me that he and Matthew were delighted to see their mom happy again. They encouraged her relationship with David. He shared what a relief it was to them to see the joy and excitement come back to Jane's life.

John and Matthew were what can be described as promoters.

I could see how various things impacted the adult children's outlook on their mom and David's relationship. But there seemed to be three primary factors that tipped the scale one way or the other: closeness with their mom, their own personal family situations, and where each was in their career.

In the past, Tom had shared that he struggled for his mother's praise. Moving several states away didn't help their relationship one bit. Michelle also didn't live anywhere near her mom. Tom and Michelle would be quick to acknowledge that, of all four siblings, they kept in touch with Jane the least.

Add to that the fact that these two had troubled marriages—Tom having just gone through a nasty divorce—and it becomes clear that the detractors' insecurities weren't caused by David. Instead, they were rooted in their own challenges and lack of fulfillment.

It wasn't surprising at all that these two were distrusting of a new companion.

As for the promoters, John and Matthew, both had steady long-term careers, one as a teacher, the other as an entrepreneur. They felt fulfilled at work and safe and connected in their marriages. This sense of safety and contentment is the antidote for insecurity and the negative emotions and behaviors that come with it.

Sadly, the negativity of detractors often wears others out. It certainly did with Jane and David. Not having the support of all her children led to Jane and David ending their relationship. And without a companion to share experiences with, Jane even quit traveling.

Years later, Jane simply isn't the same. Her health has declined, she's showing symptoms of depression and cognitive decline, and her zest for life has all but fizzled out.

||||||||||||

Jane's situation caused me to reflect on whether I've sufficiently communicated to my children my desires if I predecease my wife.

Do they know I understand the need for companionship and connection? Whatever my wife decides after my death, I fully support! After all, I know her well enough to be certain that Jill wouldn't make any rash decisions. I hope she meets a great companion with whom to spend the remainder of her life.

As for our finances, we've built our assets and retirement funds together, and of course I'd love to spend those resources with her. But if I am not here to do so, my wish for Jill is to enjoy them, and for her to love the final years of her life!

It is hard to think about and even harder to talk about, but if I don't, how would my children react? Would they be suspicious, jealous, and unsupportive? Do they know that I think they are enough, and I love them unconditionally and support them? Those are some of the questions that have been mulling around in my mind.

As stated earlier, as a culture we do not spend enough time communicating our wishes and dealing with the emotional aspects of inheritance and wealth.

To your children and grandchildren, knowing they will have enough assets after you are gone is important. More than that, they need to know that *they are enough*, that their achievements are enough, and best of all, that they can be secure knowing that their relationship with you is solid. They need to know they are pleasing to you as their parents.

While it may seem elementary, even adult children need and want to be accepted and praised by their parents. Just like Tom struggled for Jane's praise, even adult children want to please their parents and make them proud. This is as true at age eight as it is at 40.

Several of the principles discussed in this book can help nurture a sense of belonging—having a common purpose as a family, sharing your story, and forging traditions can all make your children feel like they belong. But these all flourish in a safe environment.

When you can guide your children from insecurity to confidence, it helps to prepare for inevitable changes to family chemistry, the death of a loved one, marriage, remarriage, and new generations coming of age. It may help to see a sense of belonging and acceptance as the emotional body armor to prepare for all of this, and for eventual family skirmishes.

All families have battles. Help yours avoid a war.

Avoid Fear Tactics

"Complex estate planning with its layers and layers of entities and trusts does not equate to a message of love, trust, and belonging."

Read that again and let it sink in. It's a quote from a seasoned estate attorney whom I have known for a long time. He works exclusively with clients who have a net worth greater than $50 million. I wanted to know his perspective on why so many families suffer with conflict after the death of the parents. That quote was his answer.

I agree that, especially in families with a high net worth, we put too much emphasis on the legal and tax part of planning and not nearly enough on the personal elements.

In their book *Wealth 3.0*, James Grubman, Dennis T. Jaffe, and Kristin Keffeler discuss a dynamic shift in wealth management. They address the fear tactics that are often used by advisers to move clients to action. The authors suggest a conscious shift away from what they describe as "the sales-driven approach in which surfacing or reinforcing a client's worries is the best way to engage the client."[44]

It's fair to assume we've all experienced fear-driven sales tactics. We may have even used them . . . In fact, during various

---

44 James Grubman, Dennis T. Jaffe, & Kristin Keffeler. 2023. *Wealth 3.0 The Future of Family Wealth Advising*. Family Wealth Consulting.

training programs early in my career, I was taught that fear is a great motivator.

From a financial adviser's perspective, we're all motivated to grow our book of clients. For many, if fear gets clients to listen and eventually move their legal matters, risk management, or financial assets to them, the adviser would be all the more motivated to use fear to their advantage.

This tactic is so common, after a few years into their career, advisers don't even know they are doing it.

I refuse. I have found trust to be a far better way to do business.

Where fear is used as a motivator, these are the messages you hear:

- **Fear of Missing Out** | "If you don't invest with us, you'll miss market upside."
- **Fear of Loss** | "If you don't invest with us, you won't have downside protection," or "Buy this product to insure you never have a loss."
- **Fear of Squander** | "Your children will blow everything you have worked so hard to create," or "Your child's marriage will likely end in divorce and their spouse will take part of their inheritance," or "Your children are not equipped to handle this money. It should be held in trust forever."
- **Fear of Property Loss** | "At your net worth, everyone is out to get you," or "You must ensure against every possible liability."
- **Fear of Inflation or the Devaluation of Assets** | "You have to take a risk with your investment portfolio in order to maintain the relative spending value of your portfolio."

- **Fear of Taxes** | "Create this structure or buy this product because it is tax efficient."

In the next chapter, we'll discuss family communication as the final principle for successful weather transfer. Deliberately overcommunicating your estate plan and all its parts helps squash some of these fears and softens the edges for your beneficiaries.

Communicating your plan and letting your heirs know they are unconditionally loved and appreciated for who they are seem so simple, but few families emphasize the security and confidence of the future recipients once the estate plan has been drawn up.

Familiarity with what they stand to inherit reinforces that you love and trust them, they are enough, and they belong. With each conversation comes feelings of safety and security.

Marrying Into Money

Coming from vastly different economic backgrounds is a common source of conflict between spouses and often brings tension to families.

Consider the pressure put on the spouse of an inheriting child—a son- or daughter-in-law—who does not come from money. They, too, need to feel secure and safe. They also need to feel they belong, that they are enough regardless of their upbringing. Sadly, they often don't feel that way.

Remember Brian and Dana Montgomery's story from Chapter 3, when the daughter-in-law created so much legal stir after her in-laws died? The same was also true for Todd and Judy Fenton.

Todd Fenton married into the Asher family, a family that made its fortune in the newspaper business. James, the patriarch, started as a printer at the local paper. Years later, he bought the paper from the founder, and as the paper grew, he purchased seven more daily newspapers. Eventually, he consolidated the eight papers into one large conglomerate.

When, at the start of the '90s, digital news offered the greatest challenge to the print newspaper business, James pivoted fast enough to avoid the eventual downfall of many of his competitors.

He was a no-fuss, dynamic, and highly successful entrepreneur. He was also strong-willed and disciplined all the way to the end of his life.

But for all he was, James wasn't a guy who showed much emotion. And in my 20 years of working with James, I never felt the personal closeness I often feel with clients. The same was true for his son-in-law, Todd. He never felt close to James, either.

Todd met Judy while they were still in college. And when Judy brought him home to meet her family, he was blown away. He knew Judy was from a wealthy family, but he had no clue to the extent of her family's wealth!

Imagine him arriving at their waterfront home during his first visit. The Ashers had several boats, and during that long weekend, they enjoyed hours of water skiing. When they weren't on the water with Judy's two sisters, the young couple was horseback riding through the groomed trails on the property after which they'd head home for a meal prepared by the private family chef—quite the contrast to the dining hall food Todd was accustomed to at college!

Todd laughed when he told me the story of that trip to meet the family. We met shortly after he and Judy got married. James had asked me to help "the kids" organize their estate-planning documents and life insurance.

Over the years that followed, I got to know Todd well, and during one particularly challenging season, he confided in me that he still felt like an outsider. It didn't help that his father-in-law was constantly challenging him to start a business or do something entrepreneurial.

To James Asher, it made no sense that his son-in-law could be satisfied being a teacher.

Judy opted to be a stay-at-home mom and raise their four children. Her dad didn't hide his disappointment with that choice, either. He didn't hold back on comparing Judy with his other two daughters who owned businesses.

James thought he was motivating Judy and Todd with his comments; instead, his words were demoralizing and fueled deep insecurities within the Fentons.

Once James passed away, his assets were divided equally between his three daughters. What followed blew my mind. Judy and Todd immediately hired a lawyer to challenge the distribution of assets.

The Fentons argued that the family waterfront home was rightfully theirs since they lived nearby and spent the most time there. In addition, they asked for a lump sum of additional assets to maintain the home. After all, as a teacher and stay-at-home mom, they didn't feel they'd have the capital to maintain it.

As absurd a claim as it was, after four years of bitter battles in and out of court, Judy's sisters grew tired of the legal conflict and the associated costs. They agreed to transfer the family home to Judy and Todd as part of Judy's portion of the estate. The sisters also agreed to transfer $500,000 each from their inheritances to Judy.

What might seem like a win to the Fentons really was a massive loss.

The total estate was nearly $75 million after the payment of estate taxes. In other words, without a legal challenge to the estate, Judy would have received $25 million of assets. The waterfront home was valued at $14 million when her father died, so if Judy simply offered to purchase the home immediately, it would still have left her with more than enough to maintain the property.

Instead, after the protracted legal fight, Judy got the house, $11 million in cash, plus an additional $1 million combined settlement from her sisters. But she blew hundreds of thousands of dollars in legal fees and caused her sisters to do the same. They all lost four years of their lives and peace of mind, undoubtedly, to the legal battle. Worst of all, the events drove a deep and permanent wedge between the sisters.

Todd and Judy's insecurity had manifested as fear and greed. That's what insecurity does.

This underscores the importance of creating a secure environment—helping your children, their spouses, and grandchildren know that *they are enough*. That you respect each of them regardless of differences you may have. That you honor their distinct gifts and talents.

Without this reassurance, insecurity builds. And with insecurity comes the need to prove oneself.

Be intentional about identifying and reinforcing the strengths of your inheritors—verbally and in writing. To some, this might feel awkward at first. But your legacy depends on it.

Thoughts on Equality

"Fair is not always equal, and equal is not always fair." My Uncle George used to say that a lot. It is a deep thought and can be taken a lot of ways. It can also be taken out of context.

If equality or fairness is measured in dollars, they are inherently flawed. There is not a single situation I can imagine where lifetime gifts and inheritance are done with cash. Inheritance is messy. Assets are hard to value, and each family member places different values on different assets. Plus, each person has different needs and perspectives.

Equal opportunity is the answer.

Sweet Success

The Bryant family is a chocolate family. Many people love chocolate, but the Bryants take it to a whole new level.

Jacques and Sarah Bryant met on the factory floor of Evergreen Chocolates when they were in their early twenties. Each took their first job at Evergreen after high school. Sarah started in phone sales, and Jacques was hired as a line supervisor. He was responsible for keeping the confections moving through the conveyor system (picture the infamous *I Love Lucy* chocolate factory scene).

Two weeks after Jacques started, he saw Sarah for the first time as she walked by the factory window. Jacques tripped over the conveyor trying to catch a second glimpse. He was in love. It was 1951.

By 1957, before the advent of automated production lines, Evergreen Chocolates had more than 200 full-time employees. Their chocolate-covered pretzels were in such high demand, the factory ran three shifts. By then, everyone in town knew at least one person who was an employee at Evergreen Chocolates.

Meanwhile, Jacques and Sarah's "office romance" had grown into a serious relationship. Soon enough they were married. Jacques was so talented with the machinery and conveyor systems that he quickly rose up the ranks to be head of maintenance, then eventually head of operations. Meanwhile, Sarah was a natural salesperson. She was the second-best salesperson in the company—second only to Mr. Meier, the principal owner of the company.

Mr. Meier was a bachelor, had no family, and had the reputation as the most generous person in town. He was a large donor to the hospital, the library, and other institutions that enhanced life in his small town. Many of the buildings still bear his name.

In January 1969, after the busy holiday rush, Mr. Meier called Jacques and Sarah into his office—a first for such a meeting. Leading up to it, the couple was nervous and puzzled. They had no idea why they would be summoned to the corner office.

Mr. Meier didn't keep them in the dark. No sooner had the Bryants taken a seat when Mr. Meier presented them with a proposal to buy the company. He had observed their combination of talents and handpicked them to be his successors and stewards of the company.

He would finance the purchase on very favorable terms and had only two conditions: "I don't want the company to be sold or moved for at least 20 years. And I'd like to continue to test new products for the rest of my life."

The couple didn't have to think about it for long. They were unbelievably excited and knew for sure they'd take Mr. Meier up on his offer.

By that time, Jacques and Sarah had two sons, Ian and Jeff. The boys grew up in the business—literally! Sarah was so busy with her accounts, Mr. Meier had authorized the creation of a small playroom in the factory where the boys could play until they were old enough to go to school.

This inspired a company-funded nursery for all employees as a benefit that still exists today.

When Mr. Meier died in 1987, he was 96. Jacques and Sarah came up with an idea to honor Mr. Meier's memory every year on the third Saturday in July. His passion was experimenting and inventing new chocolate confections, and they wanted to create a party atmosphere where employees could relax, have fun, and maybe discover the next new bestseller. They called it "Splatter Day" and on those days, there's melted chocolate everywhere!

Splatter Day is a blast! Employees come with ideas to cover *everything and anything* in chocolate, and no idea is turned away. The Bryant boys love to reminisce about the crazy ingredients they were allowed to put through the machinery (alongside the employees) during their childhood.

One year, they had a vegetable theme. There was chocolate-covered asparagus, green beans, broccoli, and carrots that year, though none of those caught on as regular selling items.

At home, the Bryants provided every opportunity for Ian and Jeff to experiment and explore during their developmental years. They encouraged them to try different activities, music lessons, sports, and art programs.

Jacques and Sarah made it clear they supported Ian and Jeff in whichever activities they pursued as long as the boys were committed and put in the effort their coaches and teachers prescribed.

Jacques once told me, "Jeff's hockey was definitely the biggest commitment for the whole family. I'm not sure which was worse—the crazy early morning practices, or the hours spent in the hockey arenas bundled up!" And like many parents with kids in sport could attest, Jacques told me that for a solid decade, his car smelled rancid from the equipment.

As for Ian, his passion during middle school and high school was film and movie editing. This took less travel and family time than hockey, but it required a greater investment in cameras, tapes, and editing tools. One of Ian's favorite subjects to film was Jeff on the ice, playing hockey. Jeff still has the highlight reel Ian gave him for his 18th birthday.

Jacques and Sarah often shared with Ian and Jeff the notion that they support them equally, and they talked openly about the difference between an investment of time (hockey) versus the investment of dollars (film editing). "Our goal is to always treat you fairly," they assured their sons. "But fair is not always equal, and equal is not always fair."

When it came time to pick careers, it was not a surprise to anyone that Ian gravitated to film—specifically film editing. He is now a producer for a major sports network.

Meanwhile, Jeff's scars and surgically repaired joints are evidence that he played competitive hockey through high school and college. He still plays in an adult league. After college, Jeff took a job with the local hockey team, an affiliate of the National Hockey League. He worked hard toward his goal of becoming a general manager for a hockey team. But after six years on what he thought would be his dream job, Jeff approached his parents asking if he could come to work at Evergreen Chocolates.

Jeff's time with the hockey club wasn't what he expected. Despite his hard work and long hours, he was not seeing any career progression. He wanted to be making bigger decisions—or at least *be in the room*—when player trades and strategy were being discussed. Instead, he was relegated to mundane support roles.

Jacques and Sarah were thrilled one of their sons might be interested in a career at Evergreen. They were also hesitant and scared. They had seen family businesses be turned upside down with a transition to a new generation of leadership. Over the next three months and with the help of a family business consultant, Jacques, Sarah, and Jeff created a plan. The plan included clear expectations, performance milestones, and a potential pathway to succession of leadership and of the business equity.

All along, Ian was part of the succession conversation. This was a suggestion from the business consultant.

The reality was that the family's single-largest asset was Evergreen Chocolates. Even though Ian had no interest in being involved in taking it over, everyone felt it was important he had a seat at the table, could ask questions, and would support the plan. Thankfully, Ian was, in fact, supportive of his brother and thrilled he would be taking over the family business.

In 2016, Jacques died. He was 87. Just seven months later, aged 85, Sarah also passed away. Ian and Jeff say their mom died of a broken chocolate-covered heart.

As for Jeff, he has done an unbelievable job growing the company. Today, it is one of the largest national private-label, enrobed-chocolate suppliers. The company has almost doubled in worth since Jacques and Sarah's deaths and has solid growth plans.

I am fortunate to have a front-row seat to the impact Ian and Jeff's career choices have had on their personal finances. Ian makes a great living as a producer, but without equity in Evergreen, his net worth is approximately 30% lower than that of Jeff.

At my most recent meeting with Ian, I asked him a very delicate question: "Do you ever regret not being part of Evergreen?"

"Are you kidding?" he responded. "I love what I do. I can't picture how different my life would be if I stayed at home to work at Evergreen. I think I'd be miserable. But I get to come and enjoy Splatter Day every year!"

I shared I had seen other families torn apart with these types of scenarios. "How is it that your family's different?"

Ian got serious. "I know Mom and Dad were careful to leave me an equal share of their assets when they died. My family and I have more than we need. More importantly, *I had every opportunity that Jeff had to join the family business.* I was part of the conversations when Jeff started there, and I knew it wasn't for me."

Jacques and Sarah created a safe environment for Ian and Jeff throughout their formative years. They allowed for free expression, experimentation, and exploration. The result is evident: two children pursuing separate passions while having a beautiful, non-resentful, non-competitive relationship.

Counselor's Insights

To feel safe, we have to trust our needs will be met, that our well-being—and all things that protect our well-being—isn't threatened. This is a basic truth related to our survival. Below is a quick summary of the stories in this chapter.

Two of Jane Green's children, John and Matthew, felt safe and not threatened by her relationship with David. But due to their life circumstances, her other children, Tom and Michelle, didn't feel safe. They didn't trust their mom had their well-being in mind when she started dating David.

Judy Fenton's sisters felt secure and safe in their relationships and financial situations. But Judy and Todd felt threatened when Judy's parents died, and they questioned whether their lifestyle could be maintained.

Finally, Jacques and Sarah Bryant were able to instill a sense of safety in both their sons, Ian and Jeff, despite their very different career paths and involvement in the family business. How did Jacques and Sarah accomplish this? There are several contributing factors.

We will focus here on one aspect of safety we can control and promote during the wealth transfer process—being regulated around the topic of inheritance. It's best seen in something called the **polyvagal theory**.

This theory is based on the neuroscience of the brain and its connection to the body's nervous system. The theory helps us understand how vastly differently we process and react to things based on what part of our brain we're operating out of.

When we operate from our prefrontal cortex, we are at "the top of our system" where we have access to executive function, can use reason, can solve problems, and can communicate effectively. As a result, we feel safe.

As we become increasingly distressed or feel our safety is threatened, we revert and "travel down the ladder" of the polyvagal system. This means we are operating from the back sections—or pre-historic area—of our brain. This physical area of our brain operates in the *fight or flight* mode. When excessively distressed, our brain operations move into the dorsal or *freeze* mode.

Healthy decisions—ones that foster connection and compromise—are rarely, if ever, made from the lower parts of our brain.

And here's the kicker: we literally *cannot* be in two parts of our brain at once. So, when you head into fight, flight, or freeze, executive functions and problem-solving are no longer possible.

What could have prevented Tom and Michelle Green and Judy and Todd Fenton from moving into a fight or flight mode? What may have helped them and what could similarly help you is to focus on factors you can influence. Recognize that your influence and your message are most important to your heirs. In the process, provide them with as much regulation and calm as possible.

Take advantage of doing this while you are still living. Model wise and calm perspectives about wealth to help regulate and ground your family around the topic of inheritance. Don't be afraid to discuss inheritance. Shying away will signal danger for those around you.

Our nervous systems communicate and influence one another. This is especially noticeable in airports—there's an omnipresent buzz coming from everyone's nervous systems being at a heightened state. And systems talk to systems, exacerbating the nervous energy and stress that seem to define air travel.

The same is true when it comes to how your family communicates. Your presence along with everyone's inclusion at initial discussions of wealth and inheritance allows you to establish a tone of safety. It helps ground your whole family.

Jacques and Sarah clearly did an optimal job of exposing both of their sons to their regulated, calm, and safe attitude associated with wealth transfer.

Tangible Tools for Creating a Safe Environment

- **Start now.** Ideally, start while at least one parent is still present and can positively impact the process.
- **Regulate.** Wealth creators are typically more regulated around the topic of inheritance. So, pass on your feelings of safety and calm.
- **Check in with your emotional state.** If you notice any clues that you don't feel regulated or safe, seek counsel and do the necessary work to achieve a regulated state.
- **Use a neutral location.** This also allows perceived power and influence to be neutralized and increases the likelihood of all parties feeling on equal footing. This, in turn, allows them to feel safe and stay regulated.
- **Intentionally include all parties.** Inclusion induces a sense of belonging and safety.

In Short | Show your inheritors you trust them. Let them know they're enough just as they are. Intentionally reinforce that you are proud of them and that you support them. This will help those who are feeling insecure feel confident with what they bring to the table.

You may have noticed a common thread among the positive stories you have read so far. The inheritors who were best equipped to handle the next phase of their lives had frequent, open, and transparent communication with their parents. That's the final principle, the one we'll turn to next.

9

Overcommunicate

Your beliefs become your thoughts.
Your thoughts become your words.
Your words become your actions.
Your actions become your habits.
Your habits become your values.
Your values become your destiny.
~Mahatma Gandhi

Whenever I am traveling and people ask where I'm from, I tell them Philadelphia, but really, I grew up 20 miles east, in Medford, New Jersey, also known as "South Jersey."

South Jersey is mythical. There is no delineation between South, Central, and North Jersey, but it's

Principle 9:
Overcommunicate
Destructive Emotion:
Fear
Constructive Emotion:
Courage
Proposition:
Transparency is key.

what we call it. South Jersey is where we call going to the beach "going to the shore."

Being a born and bred South Jersey boy, you can imagine my excitement about my very first business meeting in Philadelphia. I was just 23 at the time, and I was Uncle George's trainee—or more accurately, his bag handler and chauffeur.

I had driven through Philadelphia hundreds of times and been to dozens of pro sports games in South Philly. But I had never spent time in the business district, let alone inside any of the skyscrapers of downtown Philadelphia.

Perhaps you can imagine how overwhelming it was for me to walk into One Liberty Place, the tallest building in Philadelphia at the time. I was dressed for the part: blue suit, crisp white shirt, tie, my new shoes so shiny I could see my reflection. But I was incredibly nervous and felt totally out of place, wondering if folks could see that I really didn't belong.

My palms must have been sweaty when I first shook Tim Collins's hand. His company, Collins Waste Management (CWM), was the largest waste hauler in the mid-Atlantic region. His was the company everyone was talking about. CWM was growing fast, had a great reputation throughout the region, and had just gone public on the New York Stock Exchange.

Tim was "the man," a vision of success.

It was clear to me from the start that Tim was super smart. He had built his waste removal empire from scratch, yet he was one of the most calm, humble, kindhearted men you'd ever meet. His skill in managing people and acquiring smaller companies was matched only by his ability to tell the most interesting stories about his time serving in the US Army during the Vietnam War.

Over the years and with our guidance, Tim and his wife, Shelley, had done a lot of intentional estate planning. They had set up two trusts and a family partnership dating back to the early 1990s.

The guiding principle was always the same: equal treatment for their three children. But as you may recall my Uncle George saying: "Fair is not always equal, and equal is not always fair."

Fast forward to 2009, Tim and Shelley were now in their 80s. Their oldest and youngest children were married, had established careers, and were juggling the joys and responsibilities of raising their own children.

But when it came to their middle child, Scott, things had turned out a little differently. Scott had fallen in love with and married Leah, who fell hard into drug addiction. Their marriage was rocky from the beginning, and after Leah became pregnant, things kept getting worse. Leah was unable to deal with the stress of motherhood and moved out of the house shortly after the birth of their son. Scott was left to raise his son alone.

Even with repeated attempts to help Leah in recovery, her constant relapses continued, resulting in property theft and violent behavior toward the entire family. Scott was able to have a judge sign off on a divorce, but since Leah would not cooperate in the legal process, this final step had to wait until they had been separated for two years.

Safe to say, Leah was universally detested by the family.

Raising a child as a single parent made it hard for Scott to establish a career, especially one who would support a lifestyle his parents had hoped for him. Tim and Shelley supported Scott by buying a home where he and his son could live rent free.

Allowing Scott to live without paying rent is an IRS no-no. In a case like this, the IRS considers the fair market value of rent to be a gift. And gifts in excess of the IRS-defined annual exclusion require the filing of a gift tax return—something the Collins couple had not done.

Tim, Shelley, their attorney, and I brainstormed solutions and concluded that the best way to mitigate taxes was to transfer the house to Scott. And even though Scott and Leah were divorced, Tim and Shelley wanted to provide creditor protection and be extra sure Leah could never lay claim to the house. The attorney determined it would be safest for Scott to use a trust.

But Tim and Shelley were also concerned about their goal of equality among their children. How would a gift of a $400,000 home resonate with Scott's brothers?

I suggested we call a family meeting. At first, Tim and Shelley had reservations. They were concerned such a meeting could be disruptive and feelings would be hurt.

I encouraged them to consider the pros and cons and to take the risk. "Allowing the boys to be mad or uncomfortable while you're alive is far better than letting them deal with confusion or uneasy feelings after you're gone," I explained.

They saw the logic in my argument and asked if I'd be available to facilitate the meeting. I had known the family for a long time, so it was an honor to be asked and an easy yes. But with their sons spread out across the country, we decided it would be easiest to host a video conference.

Their son Bobby lived nearby and had taken on the role as Tim and Shelley's de facto caregiver, so he would be with them for the call.

Tim and Shelley wanted to rehearse what we'd be discussing during the meeting and be sure their messaging was clear. This was a great idea. We planned a call for just the three of us a week before the family meeting. Being able to go over what they would say helped them feel more confident that the outcome of the call would be positive.

Not surprisingly, the Collins couple felt it necessary to warn me about how they thought each of their adult children would react—a perfectly natural part of mental preparation.

On the day of the meeting, I woke up very anxious, wanting the call to be as perfect as it could be. (Jill told me I was emotionally invested in this family, and she was right. It was a good reminder to me to keep my professional demeanor in check and not let my personal feelings get in the way.)

At 3:00 p.m., their oldest son, Chris, along with Scott logged on for the video conference, but Tim, Shelley, and Bobby were running late. Bobby had gone to their house early to assist his parents with getting the video set up and the connection to work, but it turned out to be more of a technical challenge than they expected.

They tried to solve the problem by connecting via voice only, but they couldn't get the audio to work. Next, they tried a different computer, but the video kept freezing, and we could only hear every other word.

Bobby finally solved the technical problems, and we started the call about 10 minutes late, which feels like forever when it comes to troubleshooting connecting to a video conference.

Why do I share these details? It's important to know going into a family meeting that there will likely be glitches, that things may not go exactly as planned.

Fortunately, rather than getting frustrated, Chris and Scott exhibited patience and empathized with the connectivity issues. By the time Tim, Shelley, and Bobby were on the video conference, everyone was just grateful the issues had been resolved, and they were ready to have an open conversation.

As the facilitator, I reminded myself I didn't have to be the *smartest* person in the room, I just had to *be in* the room to create accountability and foster open communication.

I opened the meeting by first welcoming everyone and commending them on their openness in supporting the family goals. Next, I presented some background on gift tax rules and our agenda.

Tim was next on the agenda. "Mom and I have always said we want you to be treated equally," he reminded their three sons. "It's important for you to know this. We've been very careful over the years to equalize our gift giving."

With a slight tremble in his voice, Tim went on to remind them that Scott's situation was out of the ordinary. "We all know Leah and the stress she's put on this family. As Mom and I have shared with you separately, we have set up a trust for Scott. We believe it's the right thing to do. We'll also continue to work with our attorney to provide an equalization formula under our wills."

I was so proud of Tim for the way he addressed his and Shelley's mortality along with the obvious truth—Leah is a potential legal problem, and Scott needs ongoing legal protection. He had chosen his words carefully and had rehearsed them.

The next part, though, was unscripted.

Chris and Bobby beautifully expressed their selfless support for their brother. Chris said he'd be willing to inherit less so that Scott could be more comfortable. And Bobby asked if there were other creative gifting ideas to make sure Scott and his son had ample support—even if it decreased his own inheritance.

As for Scott, he was embarrassed by the attention and outpouring. He hated being a burden and insisted he didn't need the house. "Can't we just sell it?"

Shelly had anticipated this reaction, predicting the week before during our rehearsal call that Scott would object.

In the presence of everyone, Shelley acknowledged Scott's feelings. She made it clear, though, that putting the home in a trust was the right thing to do. The family agreed. Shelley complimented Scott on how he navigated being a single father and expressed her gratitude for his frequent visits with his son as she and Tim grew older.

Tim and Shelley, each in their own words and ways, were able to let their sons know exactly what to expect, and in doing so, they modeled transparency and mutual respect.

The meeting was a resounding success. The only thing that could have made it better would have been to have it in person rather than on video so the family could go out for a nice dinner together afterward. That way, they could celebrate being united as a family, having each other's unwavering support.

Being united as a family indeed is worth celebrating. Not all families are as united, as you'll see in the following story.

An Information Vacuum

No one saw it coming.

John Garcia was killed in a hit-and-run while biking on a rural road near the coast of California. By the time some surfers passed by and saw the body, it was too late to save him.

Losing a loved one is disturbing no matter the circumstances. But when he's still in his late 50s, an avid triathlete, and super wealthy, the loss is even harder to process.

If John knew what lay ahead for his family, he undoubtedly would have clearly communicated his wishes. But he hadn't.

John was a planner. He came into the marriage with a net worth of more than $24 million. And he and his wife, Theresa, accumulated several vacation properties in Malibu, dreaming of the day when they would spend summers out west with all their kids and grandkids at their "happy place."

John loved his family. He and Theresa recently celebrated their fifteenth wedding anniversary. Both had a child from an earlier marriage, and they added a set of twins to make the perfect arrangement of "yours, mine, and ours." Not that they made that distinction. Theirs was a cohesive family with all four children treated the same.

John also loved his job running a distribution and warehousing company. The company was thriving after five years of his ownership. He enjoyed managing all the complicated dynamics of the various customer and stakeholder needs.

And when he needed to clear his head, John would go running, biking, or swimming. He was keen on completing the Iron Man triathlon at Lake Tahoe later that year.

But then the accident happened. For his family and the company, the days and weeks after John's sudden death were horrible.

As John's long-time trusted financial advisor, I was relieved that he had updated his will and estate plan six years earlier. John's attorney had helped him and Theresa set up several trusts and new wills. This was the first time John's will included his stepdaughter—Theresa's daughter from her prior marriage—as an equal inheritor.

I traveled to the Garcia home for a meeting with Theresa a few weeks after the funeral. Uncharacteristically, the house was a mess. I had to clear space at the dining table for my paperwork.

Theresa talked non-stop, but not everything made sense as she had hardly slept since the day she got the fateful call.

She was clear about one thing, though: she would do whatever it took to maintain family harmony. She was especially concerned for John's daughter, Sharon. And she wondered about the future of the family company.

Despite her emotional state, Theresa's instinct was to be the best possible steward of their assets. This is where the rub came in.

According to John's will, the assets were all Theresa's for her lifetime—including the more than $24 million John brought into the marriage, which had since almost doubled. Once Theresa passed, everything would be divvied up equally between the children. Until her death, the CFO of John's company was appointed as the trustee and would oversee the management of the trust assets.

The plan for the assets was drawn up in private, and no one except John's attorney knew exactly how they'd be distributed. John's sudden death changed that.

Theresa explained that while she tried to protect family harmony, Sharon wasn't hiding her anger about "sharing *her* money" with her stepmom, half-siblings, and her stepsister. And having a trustee who would be overseeing her future inheritance made things even worse for her.

I listened as Theresa poured out her heart, and in the months that followed, I assisted her with the all-consuming administrative burdens of settling the estate—retitling properties and investment portfolios into the trusts and helping to gather the information her attorney needed to file the estate tax return.

In the years following John's passing, I observed Theresa's unconditional support of each of the young-adult children. She offered emotional support where she could, and she freely paid for college, graduate school, weddings, and mental healthcare.

Whatever support the kids needed, they got it. No matter if the child was John's, Theresa's, or theirs together, Theresa was committed to impartiality.

The same could be said of the trustee, John's former CFO. He was professional, communicative, and seemed like a great fiduciary. He went above and beyond the typical trustee duties to help navigate the complexities of this blended family.

But after a couple of years in this role, that CFO became increasingly concerned about the undercurrents of discontent from Sharon and stepped down from his role as trustee.

That's when the Garcias asked my very close friend Bruce to be the successor trustee. Bruce is an accountant and serves as trustee for many high-net-worth families. I recommended him to Theresa when she was searching for a replacement.

Bruce knew one of the best things he could do right off the bat would be to build relationships with each of the children, seeing that he hadn't met them before. He wanted them to know that he would be an impartial fiduciary and would carry out the terms of the trusts. He asked to have a family meeting where he could get to know everyone.

They agreed the meeting would be at their vacation home in Malibu. According to Bruce, they started the weekend together with Friday night cocktails, followed by a wonderful dinner looking out on the water. Bruce could easily see why this had been John and Theresa's happy place.

While Bruce was serving himself a cocktail and taking in the beautiful sunset through the large kitchen window, Sharon cornered him. She didn't mince words when she let Bruce know that it wasn't fair that her step- and half-siblings and stepmom were sharing in *her* inheritance. Her emotion was palpable, she was radiating anger and deep contempt for her stepfamily.

I believe that Sharon was not only grieving the loss of her father but also her perceived loss of inheritance and control. It is also likely that she was seeking respect and was questioning her role in the family.

After Bruce's interaction with Sharon during cocktails, everyone met at the dining room table to formally discuss the various trusts that were formed under John's will and the investment strategy for each. Most importantly, they talked about Theresa's desire to keep the family relationships strong and her goal to treat each member of the family the same, regardless of birth parent.

Afterward, everyone mingled for a few hours, sharing and laughing at old family stories, like about the family vacation to the Grand Canyon, when their rental van broke down in the middle of nowhere.

Overall, the meeting accomplished the goals Theresa laid out with Bruce: open the lines of communication and build relationships.

Sharon wasn't easily appeased, though. In hindsight, Bruce says he should have seen right then that Sharon would cause problems for him like she did for the first trustee. She became a frequent, outspoken critic of the legal structure which was dictated by her father's will.

At first, Bruce would get polite calls from Sharon to check in on the assets and investment performance. There would be cursory discussion about strategy, requests for copies of legal documents, and clarifying the trust terms. It was clear to Bruce that Sharon was building a legal file and looking for ways to get around the legal arrangements.

As time went on, Sharon became abrasive toward her stepmom, hurling insults such as, "She's spending my inheritance!" and "She has no right to my father's assets!"—and the dreaded, "Dad would not have wanted things to happen this way."

Sharon also insisted that Theresa was favoring her biological son and the twins with annual gifts, educational support, and misusing the trust income. (Bruce never saw any evidence to support this view.)

This went on for several years and drove a wedge between Sharon and each of the other family members.

After a tremendous amount of pressure and hostility from Sharon, Theresa asked that one of the trusts be terminated. She wanted each child to inherit their portion of one of the trusts right away rather than waiting for her death—natural, or otherwise.

Each child would inherit several million dollars. Even so, Sharon kept insisting on multiple accountings and legal representation. She over-complicated what was intended to be a generous, peace-seeking offer.

In the end, terminating the trust and distributing the proceeds seemed to create a dangerous precedent and pattern of greed. Shortly after the termination of that trust, history repeated itself. At that time, Bruce made the tough decision to resign as trustee.

The family appointed a new trustee, an established trust company. Unfortunately, Sharon would later sue that company, citing misuse of funds and breach of fiduciary duty.

Try as Theresa might, fear and the complexities of their blended family created a schism that exists to this day.

What Would Have Helped?

I was told that John and his first wife had a history of challenges with Sharon as a teenager. The couple had sought therapy to help them navigate things, but it seemed to offer little resolution. Sharon had been a challenge throughout her entire young-adult life.

The fact that she continued to cause problems for trustees doesn't come as a surprise. Knowing this history helps keep perspective while encouraging extra effort—and possibly the hiring of additional counseling or facilitation professionals to help ease the family tension.

It doesn't mean you just accept that someone will resist or incite conflict. Instead, the more complicated the family dynamics, the more important it is to have clear, upfront communication.

I believe establishing family meetings when the oldest kids were in college would have bolstered the chances for this family to stay together.

"But what about Sharon's sense of entitlement?" you may ask. "Her siblings seemed to stay out of the conflict and appear to be content with what they have received."

Is it that she's greedy or entitled? Or could it be that Sharon was hurting and turning to money to address her sense of helplessness and her fears regarding future financial security? Could it be that the other siblings have better coping mechanisms to address those fears?

Regardless of the presence of some difficult personalities and complex family dynamics, *it's always better to address fears while both parents are still living.* Knowing and naming a conflict while everyone is living prepares families to diffuse conflicts after the death of a parent.

The Garcias didn't have the opportunity to establish family meetings where John and Theresa could communicate their vision for the family's wealth. Had they done so, it would have allowed everyone to feel grounded.

Instead, for Sharon, fear has manifested as greed, and it has created lasting family conflict.

Fear is a wicked emotion. In the context of family relationships, it is the opposite of feeling secure and grounded. Fear of not having enough, not belonging, or not being treated fairly are common reactions when parents die without communicating their plans and wishes.

Having sat in on countless family meetings, I have found that most family relationship conflicts are rooted in fear.

It may be counterintuitive to think someone who is about to inherit tens of millions of dollars could fear they won't have enough. Most of us cannot relate, further isolating the person who experiences such fear.

For one, the security blanket of parents always paying for things or making large gifts is about to be gone. What's more, death is the end of the road when it comes to parents compounding and growing their wealth. Instead, an inheritance is a fixed number, and the responsibility for stewardship and care of wealth irrevocably shifts to the inheritor.

I once had a client who was at the precipice of selling his company for nearly $100 million tell me about the irrational fear he was facing. "You don't understand, Sean," he told me. "I have never lived on a fixed income before."

No economic model could convince him that everything would be alright. He was mentally stuck on the idea that he would never be entitled to the terrific annual profits generated by his business.

Another fear that surfaces and is most intense at the death of parents is the fear of not belonging. Most of the time—though not always—the unconditional love between parents and their children is irreplaceable. This is especially true for an inheritor who has a strained relationship with their siblings. Without the glue of their parents' love, they no longer feel they belong in their family of origin.

The finality of death brings fear to the forefront of emotions. After parents' death, I have heard phrases like, "You were always Dad's favorite," and "Mom and Dad were always harder on me as the oldest."

Spoken or unspoken, these feelings are borne in fear and lead to conflict and strain on interpersonal relationships.

A stark contrast to fear is the feeling of courage—the antidote to fear.

Inheritors who have courage are grounded and know what to expect when their parents die. There are few surprises, and they are well prepared for what lies ahead.

Instilling courage and security requires ongoing communication and training. This helps inheritors feel secure because they have been able to ask questions and envision what life will be like when mom and dad are gone.

Creating a Family Meeting Culture

When you meet Frank Johnson, you'd never guess that he and his three younger brothers were raised by a single mom at a time when being a single mother was rare. His father abandoned them when the boys were just in elementary school.

Frank's mom wasn't afraid of working hard to provide for her boys. She instilled in her sons a value for hard work, and this led to her oldest attending Massachusetts Institute of Technology where he followed his interest in mechanical engineering.

Frank and Lori met during their freshman year at MIT where she majored in music, and they married shortly after college. They'd eventually have four boys of their own.

At work, Frank exhibited a propensity for risk-taking and engineering design. His boys were barely in school when Frank stepped out to start a small company.

During those early years, Lori offered music lessons to keep the family afloat. Soon enough, though, Frank designed some widgets that would become widely used in construction all over the world.

Within 20 years, the Johnsons' finances went from zero net worth to a true business empire with a balance sheet exceeding $75 million. Their sons were too busy with their own activities to slow down, let alone comprehend their family wealth.

I talked to the couple about the importance of communicating with their boys so they could be prepared for what lay ahead for them. When I explained the value of having regular family meetings, Frank and Lori asked me to join the meetings.

The purpose of the first meetings was to share their family philosophy and educate their sons—ranging from ages 15–21—on high-net-worth topics not typically taught in school. Topics like taking financial risks, investment philosophy, creditor protection, and how taxes work.

During the third meeting, the couple gave a full disclosure of their assets and liabilities, revealing that each of their sons would inherit more than $18 million each. Amazingly, the boys didn't express shock or surprise at the magnitude of the family holdings. It could be that they had an idea of the scale from the earlier meetings, or they could have been embarrassed to show much emotion with me in the room.

For the past 10 years, the Johnsons have continued these meetings. As the boys got married, their wives have also been invited to attend and participate in the meetings. Nowadays, these meetings are part of their greater family culture.

Through it all, the Johnsons have created a beautiful cadence and balance of communication. In addition to the financial discussions, the meetings have evolved to cover vulnerable, personal, and timely topics.

I have high expectations for the transition of wealth in the Johnson family to be smooth, that they will safely navigate the successful transfer of wealth.

|||||||||||||

For the Garcias, the sudden death of the family patriarch sent everyone in the family into a tailspin, with lasting effects and conflict. Contrast that with the example my Uncle George set and what the Collins family and Johnson family embrace, and you can see why I stress the importance of family meetings.

In fact, family meetings are at the heart of successful estate planning.

This is true for both the practical transfer of assets as well as—and possibly more importantly—a smooth emotional transition.

First-generation entrepreneurs often have a hard time slowing down from the hard-charging pursuits of business. For them, it can be hard to step back and appreciate the need for succession and communication. In fact, it may even be easier to create their next company than to do the work of calling family meetings to educate the next generation, share values, and facilitate a successful wealth transfer.

Many of them don't even have a will—which is essential—let alone a full estate plan.

The Importance of a Will and Estate Plan

It never ceases to amaze me, but not everyone I meet has written a will. Either they are too busy, as mentioned above, or they just don't want to deal with their own mortality. And some have an aversion or fear of discussing the topic of what happens after we die.

Plus, there are those who somehow want to believe they will never die . . . With them, bringing up the subject can be uncomfortable, to say the least. At death, a clear, well-thought-out will and an estate plan—an overall plan for the disposition of assets, including trusts and other legal entities—create the framework to carry out your wishes.

Except in the case of a premature death, when donors have not had the opportunity to establish a philosophy and precedent for communication, **the contents of the estate plan should not come as a surprise to any of the beneficiaries or fiduciaries.** This stresses the importance of open communication during family meetings.

A First Family Meeting

Kenneth Nero had already proven himself in the world of real estate development when he met and married Louise. It didn't take long before their company was known as the one to turn to for the largest real estate deals in the Midwest.

The couple had one son, Joe, and five years later their daughter, Sue, was born. With the five-year age gap, the siblings were never particularly close, but they got along fine.

Joe, in his early thirties, was a registered nurse at the Mayo Clinic. He was clear about what he wanted in life and was well on his way to achieving his goals, including planning on proposing to his girlfriend of several years.

Sue, on the other hand, was single and spending all her time growing her wedding photography business. It was far from thriving, but Sue did well enough to make her mortgage payment and live a simple life. Still, she was determined to keep growing her business, and she dreamed of the day she would have a large team that could shoot the biggest weddings in town.

When Kenneth and Louise sold their business in their early 60s, I helped them to set up lifetime trusts for their children. The goal of the trusts was twofold: it would supplement the adult children's incomes, and it would provide for creditor protection and lower the estate tax exposure of the Nero's estate when they die.

Of course, I recommended—maybe insisted—that they have a family meeting to help Joe and Sue understand the implications of the trusts and help educate them on how to manage the money that would be coming their way soon. Especially since they had no inkling of how their lives were potentially about to change once they started getting payments from their trusts.

Kenneth, Louise, and I met to map out a series of meetings. Louise couldn't hide how thrilled she thought the kids would be with the news and how grateful she thought they'd be.

From experience, though, I know it doesn't always work that way. Adult children often respond very differently than we might expect. (Think, for example, of the Johnson boys' neutral response.)

I helped both parents adjust their expectations of the meetings, especially the first one where we'd simply explain the concept of gifting and trusts—how trusts work and why they are used.

During that meeting, we had a great discussion, giving the parents and me the confidence that Joe and Sue would indeed understand the magnitude and meaning of the gifts that they would be receiving.

During our second meeting a few weeks later, the Neros revealed that each child's trust would have $4.5 million, some of which could be accessed immediately. Their uncle would be the trustee.

I loved observing the gratitude and appreciation expressed during that meeting. Both Joe and Sue were speechless at first, but it didn't take long before reality set in and they lavished gratitude upon their parents. (Turned out Louise was right about how thankful they'd be.)

Sue was a little concerned, though. She wondered if her parents would have enough left to enjoy their retirement. Of course, Kenneth and Louise assured her that they had enough to do all they had dreamed of, and more.

It was also an honor to witness the parents expressing their pride in both Joe's and Sue's accomplishments. The children both promised to be responsible stewards of the assets, which they have indeed been.

Today, the Neros would attest to the benefits of creating the trusts and communicating clearly about the purpose and design of such gifts. Had they not done so, it could have left the children wondering if their parents didn't trust them. Otherwise, why didn't they just give them the money directly?

It could have also led to friction with their uncle who had been assigned the trustee. And, as I've seen in some families, it could have led to a lack of motivation and a resistance toward continuing to work. After all, why would you have to work when you have millions at your fingertips?

Since those first meetings, the Nero family has continued to have regular, formal family meetings. Sometimes, they invite me to help facilitate. Other times, they invite their attorney or accountant as a special guest. The family has done a terrific job of keeping lines of communication open with their children, and family meetings are now part of their family culture.

Last year, the Neros even developed this family mission statement: "Our family mission is to leave the world better than we found it. This starts with an emphasis on the education and well-being of our family and continues with our community and helping those in need."[45]

Communication Styles

Regardless of the legal structures and complexity involved with an inheritance, the single most important element to a successful transfer of wealth I have observed is good communication.

Generally, communication styles and comfort with talking about personal topics—particularly finances—fall within generational categories.

Tim and Shelley Collins' discomfort talking with their adult children about their inheritance is often true of their generation of baby boomers. They see personal topics as private and are generally reluctant to share personal financial information with their children.

Generations X, Y, and Z, however, are progressively more open to discussing money and other topics which may have been taboo to their parents and grandparents.

Age isn't the only factor when it comes to how open people are to talking about money. It has been my experience that where people live plays a role in shaping their cultures and norms.

Generally speaking, folks from the southern and western states of the US are more laid back than the northeastern states. This is true with how people talk, what they wear, and even how open or shut they are about discussing money.

I once had an entrepreneur disclose details of his entire financial picture during our first meeting at a crowded sushi restaurant in Texas. No kidding! I had to ask him to lower his voice because

---

[45] Refer to Chapter 1 and our website (www.TheGreatestGiftBook.com) for ideas and suggestions on identifying your family's values and writing your mission statement.

I could see other people leaning in to listen. I have never had that experience in the Northeast.

In contrast, a client in Philadelphia needed five in-person meetings before they were trusting and comfortable enough to share their financial picture with me.

|||||||||||

Regardless of your personal style, make overcommunication a priority.

Of all the principles in this book, this one is the most important. It is the foundation on which the other principles stand. Think of it as a spin on the Golden Rule. Communicate with others the way you would like them to communicate with you—clearly, and often.

Start by calling a meeting and don't give up, even if there's some resistance. Take the time to plan the meeting. Give everyone enough of a heads up so they can block the time on their schedule.

Calling a family meeting will feel weird at first, and most participants will feel awkward or nervous. But pushing through that initial awkwardness is worth it!

The process may take time, but you and your family will be glad you did it.

I am excited about what you will learn about yourself and your family members in the process. The bond formed and peace sustained through regular, organized communication are invaluable.

Getting Started with Family Meetings

An effective family meeting allows for clear communication not only from parents to children, but for **three-way communication**—parents to children, children to parents, and children to children.

For a successful intergenerational transfer of wealth, *all three parties must communicate openly and freely.* The likelihood of conflict increases if all three aren't in clear, open communication.

Communication between parents and children is obvious. What is often left out of family communication priorities is the dialogue between children. To address this, family meetings need to have room on the agenda for open discussion among children. Communication and collaboration between siblings are also encouraged through the intentional development of a common purpose.

So, how do you establish family meetings? You start with consistent, simple, organic conversations, then transition to formal family meetings.

Having regular family meetings where you instill a common vision keeps everyone grounded. It also minimizes fear-based reactions among family members.

The way family meetings play out varies from family to family, but the goal is the same: transparent communication with the reinforcement of core values, plans, and expectations.

As such, family meetings are the forum for older family members to pass along their wishes and enable a smooth transition between generations.

Family meetings are best held at least once per year and preferably in person. Everyone should attend and the host (you) needs to make it easy for everyone to participate.

Your decision to include children will need to take into consideration the age appropriateness of the topics being discussed. As made clear in earlier chapters, I also recommend including the spouses of your children at family meetings.

And I recommend having a facilitator at the family meeting. A family counselor or financial consultant trained in family meeting facilitation can bring a level of professionalism to the meeting—

and take the pressure off you. How nice it will be for you to participate rather than run the meeting.

Having a facilitator also helps keep everyone on their best behavior. They can help if someone acts out or tries to sabotage the meeting.

The Frequency of Meetings

I often get asked how often family meetings should be held. For starters, rather than feeling family meetings are something that *must* be done, consider the idea that you may be fortunate to be able to host them.

For most families, having an annual meeting is sufficient. The cadence of meeting annually brings comfort and consistency to family members and allows them to be prepared for whatever family experiences will happen throughout the year.

Keep in mind that anything worthwhile takes effort and time. This is particularly true—and often overlooked—when it comes to family meetings and growing in communicating well as a family.

It is not realistic to believe a single meeting will suffice to accomplish clear lines of communication. That is why it's paramount to exert deliberate effort to have regular meetings.

Some families choose to hold these meetings every other year, but I'd recommend not limiting meetings to fewer than that.

And however often you choose to meet, one common mistake is the expectation that a single meeting will bring everyone up to speed on the parents' goals, desires, and wishes for their family legacy. Communicating the frequency of family meetings at the outset will help manage expectations.

When and Where to Meet

Family meetings are best when everyone can attend in person rather than virtually. Video conferences are sometimes the only option; however, the level of engagement is greater when everyone's physically in one place.

Consider planning meetings around other family gatherings. The Friday after Thanksgiving, for example, or the last week of December are often good options—especially when planned well in advance.

A comfortable, professional setting as a neutral environment can sometimes be helpful. I have facilitated very productive meetings in restaurant private rooms as well as professional conference rooms.

The level of planning that goes into a meeting reflects the importance placed on the meeting itself. Traveling to a mutual, non-residential location puts everyone in a conscious, attentive, and deliberate mindset.

This is not a hard-and-fast rule, but I have observed a different level of engagement when participants are there in person rather than joining by phone or video conference. Further, the distraction and interruptions that often come with remote participation are not courteous to the rest of the participants. So, if someone cannot make it to the meeting, rather than having them join the meeting virtually, share with them the detailed meeting minutes and presentation, if possible.

If the meeting is important enough, challenge the participants to be there in person.

For example, for our investment partnership family meetings, we have those on our calendars way ahead so everyone can plan around those meetings (they're on the third Monday of the month following the end of each calendar quarter).

This has been a custom for several years. But if a conflict arises that one of us absolutely cannot resolve, we expect them to give ample notice, and we all go out of our way to find an alternative date close to the original date so we can all meet in person.

Who Should Attend

It goes without saying that all your adult children should be invited to attend. As for their spouses, I suggest they also be invited. However, this is often a very personal decision.

The dynamic of family meetings will likely change when in-laws are included, but consider their inclusion as an example of leadership, especially if you'd like them to conduct family meetings with your future grandchildren. And by including the in-laws, you share your family values and create a safe environment, as discussed in the previous chapter.

As for inviting grandchildren to family meetings, I've found the best age to introduce children to family meetings is around 14. The first few years may be awkward for them, but the privilege of attending is a meaningful milestone for them as young adults.

Topics to Cover

It's important to be clear about what you expect from the meeting, what you hope to gain. Then take small steps toward those goals through open, honest communication.

In general, I suggest focusing the first meeting on establishing your family's philosophy and values. This creates the perfect environment for creating a family mission statement. (See Chapter 1.)

Be alert during meetings for opportunities to identify or define roles for individuals around the table. (See Chapter 4.) This might be taking on a role in organizing or following up on items discussed during the meeting.

Remember to be intentional about creating an open environment for sharing. Declare the meeting space a "no judgement zone," and reinforce that open sharing is encouraged, not condemned. (See Chapter 8.)

A family meeting is also an excellent opportunity to share your family story. What struggles did you experience during your upbringing and early career? Take the opportunity to use stories to prepare your family for future obstacles. Knowing that difficulties will happen will better prepare your family when they come. (See Chapter 2.)

The Family Meeting Agenda

The first item on the agenda could always be a review and possible amendment of the family mission statement. As for the remainder of the agenda, it's wise to request input from your family when choosing the topics to discuss. This provides better participation and allows for dialogue versus one-directional preaching.

You can also foster participation by having check-ins, going around the table and having every person share something—with no requirement as to topic or content.

Also consider having an icebreaker question such as "What is something each person is proud of from the past year?"

Before burdening them with financial details, lay a foundation by helping them feel comfortable, making sure they find the meetings to be educational and for their benefit.

When do you discuss financial details? This is a complicated question and varies from one family to another. When you first hold meetings, participants can be uneasy about attending.

Details about financial abundance can be harmful to family members who are struggling with mental health, or addiction.

I recommend family members who have exhibited responsibility and some form of stability in their personal relationships and life choices be informed of their future inheritance as early as age 25.

Including heirs early in their adulthood helps them develop a healthy relationship with financial wealth and prepare for future decision-making.

A Sample Family Meeting Agenda

The family meeting agenda can take numerous forms. As with many meetings, the agenda forms an outline for discussion. Do not overcomplicate the agenda. Leave openings for discussion and dialogue. The best parts of the conversation happen in the "white space" between topics. The key is to make everyone comfortable and list the basic items you want to be sure to cover.

If you do not hire a professional facilitator, make sure someone is in charge of leading the meeting. Your primary goal is to create a trusting, open environment. You are also in charge of keeping everyone to the allotted time. If conversations go on too long for the time permitted, be prepared to say something like, "I am making a note of this, and let's be sure to talk about it between now and the next meeting."

No one likes meetings that go on longer than their scheduled time. You will want everyone to be excited to come again next time.

1. **Family Mission Statement** | Recall the family mission statement to ensure it still aligns with what is at the heart of your family.
2. **Check-ins** | Invite those in attendance to share how they are, including news on events from their lives. Make it fun and lighthearted.

3. **Current Events** | Discuss the impact of current events, how it is impacting the family, and what is happening within the family—this can be anything from world or local news, marriages, divorces, births, relocations, health updates, family business updates, or new initiatives and ideas.
4. **Lifelong Learning** | Identify topics that may be on the minds of participants. Ask, "What can we do to support you right now, at this stage of your life?"
5. **Financial Review** | Presented by you or a professional adviser. Consider having your investment adviser, CPA, financial consultant, or a facilitator be a guest for the whole meeting, or just for this portion to present a report. This allows everyone to have a clear understanding of the state of the family's finances.
6. **Charitable Giving: Review and Strategy** | This allows you to make sure your giving is aligned with your family mission and purpose.
7. **Legal Topics** | Wills, trusts, partnerships, prenuptial agreements, estate planning, taxes, etc.
8. **Next Meeting** | Wrap up, conclusion, and setting an agenda for the next meeting and comparing calendars to schedule it.

Counselor's Insights

One day about seven years ago, I pulled into the driveway and found four fluorescent traffic cones positioned in a curved line around a space on the blacktop in front of our home. In large letters written in sidewalk chalk were the words "DROP HERE" and an enormous X to mark just the right spot.

I playfully took a picture and posted it to social media with an oh-so-witty comment along the lines of, "If only *all* of my husband's communication was this clear!"

I was joking. But I was also serious.

Never in my life had I witnessed such clear and overt communication. There was no way to misread where Sean intended the landscape supply company to drop the mulch. I admired his effort at overcommunicating. Sure enough, the mulch landed in just the right place.

This chapter with its driving principle of overcommunicating provides the vehicle for all the other principles to travel on. Without clear and healthy communication, anxiety breeds and conflict festers. The relationship highway gets clogged, breaks down, and accidents occur.

We are naturally wired for survival. Anxiety has been demonized in recent years, but it is fundamental to our survival. The purpose of anxiety is to activate the body to prepare for the unknown. It heightens your senses and elevates your brain's ability to gather information.

When you don't have sufficient information about a topic, your brain tends to spin out worst-case scenarios. It does this to prepare you to survive. But your brain finds no need to prepare you for peaceful or calming anticipatory events. You don't typically experience "what if" rumination when preparing to head out to your backyard to sit in the sun and enjoy a cup of tea . . .

However, preparing for a trip to a new destination will more than likely spur regular checks of upcoming weather and internet searches of things to do or places to avoid. Anxiety instigates a gathering of information to help you prepare for the unknowns you will encounter. It's natural, normal, and even healthy when kept at functional levels.

Having regular family meetings proactively alleviates the natural and healthy response that comes with the death of a parent. Family meetings help with the questions about how your family will navigate the change. Sharing information at family meetings helps dissipate fear of the unknown by addressing these questions while the creators of the wealth are still alive.

"Clear is kind." This is a saying I often repeat when it comes to parenting and marital relationships. The clearer our communication, the healthier our relationships will be.

Clear communication takes forethought and effort. The healthier our relationships are, the more easily conflict and struggle can be navigated. Compare these statements for clarity.

"I'll be home early this evening," versus, "I'll be home by 6:00 p.m."

"I'm hoping we can spend some time together this weekend," versus, "I'd really appreciate it if you and I dedicate Saturday afternoon from around 2:00 to 5:00 p.m. to do something active outside together."

"Mom and I will leave everything to you kids," versus, "Mom and I have created a balance sheet of our assets. Using updated valuations, we plan to split the value of these assets equally among you. The vacation home will be sold when we die, and the funds included in the estate."

Clarity helps alleviate anxiety. It fosters a sense of peace and allows people to regulate. And implementing insights from the *9 Principles for Successful Wealth Transfer* helps bring that level of clarity.

Tangible Tools for Overcommunicating
- Be as clear as possible when communicating.
- As parents and elders, model vulnerability in your communication. Sharing your experiences with discomfort around death, family inheritance, or money will help alleviate the pressure to *not* have these feelings. Ironically, when you give yourself permission to feel hard feelings, those feelings tend to quiet down. On the other hand, repressing them only leads to an increase and eventual bubbling over of non-permitted feelings.
- Be comfortable with navigating conflict using "I feel . . . I need . . ." statements to support healthy communication.
- Host family meetings where you intentionally provide opportunities to communicate.
- Consider hiring a facilitator to help with family meetings. This is a great way to bring in an unbiased third party with nothing at stake in the inheritance to enhance communication.

|||||||||||||

In Short | Transparency and regular communication are key to avoiding surprises. Have regular family meetings. Doing so gives everyone confidence and the correct expectations. It also removes fear, which is toxic when settling an estate.

To ensure you have a solid understanding of the *9 Principles for Successful Wealth Transfer*, we'll do a quick recap next. We'll also address when and how you can implement these principles.

10

Overview: The 9 Principles for Successful Wealth Transfer

I believe the principles discussed in this book are more important than tax planning or the legal structuring of your estate. Let them be the underpinning of your family legacy.

Jill and I developed these principles after reflecting on the stories shared in these pages, countless other scenarios that didn't make it into the book, and interviews with inheritors. We identified the destructive emotions that underlie actions and attitudes along with the positive emotions that help overcome those. We also identified propositions behind the principles.

Based on decades of working closely with families, we have found that destructive emotions do not start at the death of the patriarch and matriarch. Instead, they fester under the surface and explode after death—creating conflict and controversy—destroying family peace. (To be sure, this book is not a thorough research study, but merely a reflection on the patterns we have observed.)

Each principle targets a specific destructive emotion—feeling jealous, shameful, lonely, contemptuous, selfish, enmeshed, greedy, insecure, and fearful. By embracing the principle, you'll go from a destructive emotion to a constructive one—feeling connected, appreciative, like you belong, respected, compassionate, independent, generous, confident, and courageous.

Furthermore, applying these principles may help you and your inheritors emotionally regulate, that is, calmly and clearly identify what you are feeling and appropriately express these feelings to maintain connection.[46]

A Recap of the Principles

1. **Develop a Common Purpose** | Foster engagement among your heirs. This will help them feel connected so they can overcome any temptation to feel jealous when they have to share an inheritance with others.
2. **Share Your Story** | Help your children and grandchildren be grounded by regularly sharing your origin story and the story of their ancestors. Reinforce the sacrifices made to establish the family legacy. Appreciating the sacrifices you and those before you have made helps inheritors overcome feeling shameful about what they receive.
3. **Forge Traditions** | Family culture shows up through your traditions. Build on the traditions you already have. Grow

---

[46] Emotions, as you may know, are complicated. We'd be amiss if we didn't point you to Brené Brown's *Atlas of the Heart* (Random House Publishing Group, 2021), an amazing guide to understanding the layered, complex meaning of our feelings and emotions. Dr. Brown's perspectives influenced our choice of emotions.

them, encourage involvement, and find ways to make more of them. Feeling like they belong prevents inheritors from acting out, even if they feel lonely once their parents die.

4. **Define Roles** | Without having responsibilities within the family and in the management of an estate, inheritors can feel contemptuous. This is a very strong emotion, which undoubtedly will lead to immense conflict once you're no longer around. Define roles for each person to perform, and practice those while you're still alive. The responsibility that comes with having roles helps each family member feel respected.

5. **Promote Humility** | If spiritual modesty is not already part of your family culture, consider using awe and wonder to stimulate compassion. Recognizing your place in the larger order of things will influence future behavior and deter selfishness.

6. **Nurture Independence** | Striving to create self-sufficient heirs is critical to peaceful intergenerational transfer of wealth. Giving your heirs the space, opportunity, and support to do things on their own, along with giving them the permission to fail helps them move from enmeshment to independence.

7. **Encourage Giving** | Giving of your time, talents, and assets alongside your beneficiaries helps model and demonstrate love and teaches generosity. It also becomes an antidote to greed.

8. **Create a Safe Environment** | Show your inheritors you trust them. Let them know they're enough just as they are. Intentionally reinforce that you are proud of them and that you support them. This will help those who are feeling insecure feel confident with what they bring to the table.

9. **Overcommunicate** | Transparency and regular communication are key to avoiding surprises. Have regular family meetings. Doing so gives everyone confidence and the correct expectations. It also removes fear, which is toxic when settling an estate.

	Principle	Destructive Emotion	Constructive Emotion	Proposition
1	Develop a Common Purpose	Jealousy	Connection	Engagement is essential.
2	Share Your Story	Shame	Appreciation	Perspective grounds you.
3	Forge Traditions	Loneliness	Belonging	Family culture is important.
4	Define Roles	Contempt	Respect	Responsibility makes a difference.
5	Promote Humility	Selfishness	Compassion	Celebrate awe and wonder.
6	Nurture Independence	Enmeshment	Independence	Growth needs space.
7	Encourage Giving	Greed	Generosity	Charity is pure love.
8	Create a Safe Environment	Insecurity	Confidence	Trust creates safety.
9	Overcommunicate	Fear	Courage	Transparency is key.

On Implementing the Principles

As a family, it would be unrealistic to implement or even review the *9 Principles for Successful Wealth Transfer* in a single year. It makes more sense to pick one principle per year to make your own. No need to address the principles in the order I presented them. Apply them as they suit your needs.

Come back to the principles as your family changes and grows. As family milestones occur—marriage, the purchase of a first house, or the birth of a new child, for example—consider discussing a few of the principles in the first family meeting that is attended by, say, a child or grandchild's new spouse. This is a great way to welcome them to the family and demonstrate the importance of family relationships.

Such a meeting would be a good time to provide perspective by sharing your story. (See Chapter 2.) Also use it as an opportunity to share some of your family's core values while revisiting and soliciting input regarding your family mission and vision (all reflected in Chapter 1).

Death and divorce are also times in a family's evolution when intentional focus on the principles is important. Your family will feel comforted when there is consistency in the reinforcement of the propositions each principle represents.

////////////

Last Thanksgiving, just as I was wrapping up writing this book, Jill and I thought it would be a good opportunity to do what I so often facilitate with my clients—and what I promote in this book as a best practice. So, we called a family meeting.

It had been over a year since our first (and until then, also last) official meeting, so before the kids came home for their break, we let them know we'd be having a family meeting and asked them to block off 90 minutes on their schedules.

As the meeting moderator, I created a quick PowerPoint to keep us on agenda.

We met at my office, and I was surprised at how nervous I was! Of course, I wanted everyone to feel comfortable and not come away feeling it was a waste of time. By the end of the meeting, I learned that I wasn't the only one who went into the meeting nervous . . .

When I had sent out the meeting request, the kids pinged back right away. "What's up? Is everything OK?!" We assured them that everything was indeed fine. "But why do we need a family meeting?"

Though I told them at the time what the meeting was about and even sent them our meeting agenda, they were convinced Jill and I had bad news to share about our health, finances, or our relationship.

Thankfully, there was none of that. We simply wanted to get all five of us around a table—and not the dinner table. We had business to discuss.

1. **Icebreaker** | We went around the table and had each person share what they were most proud of from the last year.
2. **Review** | A facilitator had taken us through a values exercise during our meeting the year before, so we provided each family member with that list, asking if there were any changes to our top five values.
3. **The Principles** | I presented a sneak preview of the *9 Principles for Successful Wealth Transfer*. Together, our family decided that the one we'd focus on for the upcoming year would be Principle 7: Encourage Giving.
4. **Support** | Using the proven, sincere, trust-building question, "How can we best support you?" led to some great conversation.

When Jill and I asked this final question, the kids all shared how supported they felt and how much they appreciated our emphasis on communication. But the best thing about the entire meeting was what happened next.

While I was packing up my laptop and everyone was tidying up their space at the boardroom table, Zach said something I hadn't heard him say before—something that took courage. "We always have such a great time when you come to visit me in New York. I'd love it if you came to see me more often."

Even now, it warms my heart that my son asked us to come visit him more often. At the same time, I couldn't help but feel a bit of guilt remembering the story I shared in Chapter 3 about the breakdown of traditions, about Mike and Sherry Smith being so busy with their company that they never visited their children—and the catastrophic consequences of that lack of connection.

Jill and I both thanked Zach for telling us how he felt. We committed to getting some dates on the calendar to make more such visits a reality.

This prompted Ryan to raise a topic he and Zach had been talking about but didn't know when to bring up, or if it would even be OK to talk about. "Dad," he said, "we've never talked about working with you at Valley Forge . . ."

It's true. We hadn't. I didn't want any of our kids to feel there was an expectation to join the family business.

"I think we'd both be interested in working here someday," Ryan told us.

Zach nodded but was quick to add, "But we don't want to be a burden. Can we talk about it?"

Of course we could! Turns out the two most important talking points of the day had never made it onto the agenda.

The final half hour of what will be the Maher annual family meeting had the biggest impact. Proof again that good things happen when everyone can get together around the table in an accepting, comfortable, trusting way.

Postscript

A New House

I dusted the snow off my shoes and hung up my winter coat, thankful to finally be in my warm office. The commute to work was one of those where you cannot take your mind off driving. The snow was still coming down, and there were more than a few cars that had slid off the highway.

My cheeks were still ice-cold and my fingers numb from the hours spent clearing our driveway when I poured a cup of coffee and settled at my desk, ready to address the items on my to-do list for that day.

My coffee was still steaming when Josey called me. She's the oldest of three children of the Roberts family whom I have advised for over a decade. Josey is an absolute delight to work with. Her humble demeanor makes me want to immediately help whenever she asks for something.

"We found a house!" she blurted out without engaging in the typical niceties at the outset of a call. "Bart and I are so excited, Sean! We want to make an offer."

I listened patiently as she reminded me that she and Bart were expecting their first child and had finally found a house that would be perfect for them and their growing family. She barely paused to breathe as she described the home and the neighborhood to me.

"See? It's perfect for us!" she continued, also not pausing for a response. "We're talking to mortgage brokers, and they need information about our financial situation. Can you help me with that, please?"

"Why get a conventional mortgage when you could streamline the process with an intra-family loan?" I wanted to know.

The Roberts family had started having semi-annual meetings since Josey was in college, and I always attended those. Long before any of the kids were in serious enough relationships to expect engagement announcements, we discussed prenuptial agreements as Josey's mom and dad were particularly concerned about legal protections for their children and the substantial assets they'd eventually inherit.

The family meetings also covered topics such as the use of debt, how the family business is run, and estate-planning concepts—including intra-family loans. Plus, it incorporated a full disclosure of family assets.

In other words, Josey and Bart could easily borrow money from her family to purchase their home.

"Bart wants us to do this on our own," Josey told me without a hint of bitterness. "This is part of what made me fall in love with him, Sean. He's independent and wants to prove we are capable."

We decided it made sense for Bart to come to my office the next week for an in-person conversation.

Josey and Bart met in college. "In a lot of ways, Bart is just like my dad," she once told me. "He's a hardworking, high-character person." After college, Bart joined the sales team at a software company.

He grew up in a middle-class family, and prior to his first formal family meeting with Josey's parents and siblings, he had never heard of trusts, partnerships, or LLCs. Bart's only legal experience was being presented with a prenuptial agreement before he and Josey got married.

During family meetings, Bart was engaged yet humble. And he had a good poker face. I can only imagine his thoughts when we discussed the tens of millions of dollars that had been amassed for Josey, her siblings, and their future children. Not once in the almost six years since Bart joined the family and its biannual meetings did I observe any look of shock or amazement at those numbers. If he had strong emotions either way, it never showed.

"How do you feel about borrowing from your in-laws?" I asked Bart when he sat down in my office the next week. I was determined to get straight to the heart of the matter—not what the different interest rates were or the formalities of getting a mortgage. What I wanted to get to was how the idea of borrowing money from his in-laws made him *feel*.

Bart admitted that getting a mortgage from a bank would be out of stubbornness. In his heart, he knew a private loan was the best option for them. He and Josey had talked about this issue at length. No matter what they decided, he knew that the family would respect them for it.

"It feels funny, even a bit uncomfortable admitting this," Bart said with a smile. "But taking out a commercial loan would be wasteful. And that goes against our family values."

It was clear that Bart knew he had a place in the Roberts family. He knew the family trusted him, that they appreciated his initiative in researching the best option for his and Josey's future family. He also knew that the two of them had been given the autonomy to make an informed decision.

"They'd never force us to take a private loan, Sean. You know it." And I did.

In the years of working with them, I had seen up close how the Roberts family created a safe environment for open discussion and decision-making. They had created a foundation of inclusion, trust, transparency, and respect. And all of this was reinforced through their family culture, which included regular, transparent meetings.

||||||||||||

Stories like that of Josey and Bart are why I wrote this book. *It's about more than just money.*

It's about love, trust, and belonging. It's about seeing, appreciating, and respecting each other for who we are. Honoring one another. Connecting well. It's about setting up our children for success that surpasses financial success, helping them live with compassion, generosity, confidence, and courage.

Periodically, check in with the *9 Principles for Successful Wealth Transfer* outlined in this book. As new members join the family or others pass away, you'll want to adapt how you implement these to give your beneficiaries the greatest gift.

About the Authors

Sean Maher has been providing financial consulting to high-net-worth families since 1996. As a Principal at Valley Forge Financial Group, Inc. and CEO of Valley Forge Family Office, Sean regularly presents to industry groups on complex estate-planning concepts.

Sean has held board positions with multiple charities. He has published articles for *Trust & Estates*, *Journal of Financial Planning*, and *National Underwriter*. Sean created the Valley Forge Practicum—a free summer seminar for high school- and college-age students interested in a career in financial services.

To clear his head, Sean swims laps—dreaming of the glory days when he was a competitive swimmer.

Sean's wife, Jill, is a licensed psychological counselor and serves clients at the Peacemaker Center, a not-for-profit mental health counseling provider. She has been a spin instructor for 22 years and has been known to "counsel from the saddle."

Sean and Jill have been married for almost 30 years and have three adult children. They are college sweethearts, having met in cooking class at Cornell's School of Hotel Administration.

The Maher family lives in Chester County, Pennsylvania. Sean and Jill relax by spending time with their children, friends, and extended family. They enjoy exploring, especially when they can combine their travel with sightseeing by bike. Their happy place is MidCoast Maine's Damariscotta Lake, where they journey each summer for family vacation.

Acknowledgments

Jill, this book would not have been written without your encouragement, support, and ongoing contribution. While you are credited for the Counselor's Insights sections, you and I know how your influence, perspective, and wisdom permeate the entire text. Thank you.

Zach, Ryan, and Kylie, thank you for being willing to let your name and experiences be used throughout. I constantly learn from you, and you enrich my life beyond measure.

Thank you to everyone who privately shared their family inheritance stories, experiences, and perspectives with me. You and your families have shown me that chaos is not inevitable when inheritance happens.

To my clients, this book attempts to relay the hard-earned insights you have shared with me over the last three decades. As business owners and heads of your families, you are leaders in your industries, influencers in business, and it is a privilege to work with you. Thank you for trusting me with your most sacred goals and objectives. You have taught me many lessons. I will not list your names here for confidentiality, but you know who you are.

I get overwhelmed thinking about the early support from Allison Hill, Matt Brosenne, Debbie Errin, Krista Gilbert, Chris Conway, Frank Michel, Fernanda and Rob Groff, Heather Moran, Rich Radnay, Robyn Maher, Jenny Mallick, Frank Sposato, Karen,

Colleen, and Kathleen Beyer, Alisa Shin, Tina Lovejoy, Leigh Segal, Steve West, Kyle West, Nancy Ingerman, Cindy Roberts, Roy Jenkins, and Mom and Dad. (Back then, the book's working title was *The Intersection of Grief and Greed*.) Your enthusiasm and your confidence in me along with your recognition of the need for this book was my motivation to keep writing.

I am eternally grateful for the mentorship of the late George C. Beyer, Jr., and Louis Paul. Their guidance and belief in me were the accelerators for my professional development.

Adéle Booysen and Karen Anderson, you are the book coaching and editing dream team. Thank you for helping me turn a very rough and choppy draft into a well-organized manuscript that will bring more peace and love to the world.

Cameron Maher, the cover design is fantastic! Camille Aman, thank you for helping me navigate marketing, the website, and social media.

Mike Maher, Mike Mallick, Steve Mumford, Trina Menta Hanna, Mike Creighton, and all my current and former colleagues and friends at Valley Forge Financial Group, thank you for embracing wholistic and purposeful planning for our clients. I am grateful to be part of such a wonderful company.

So, What Now?

This is your call to action. *Now* is the time to get started so you can give your family *the greatest gift* of a successful transfer of wealth.

If you're already incorporating some of the principles of this book, look at some of the others. Have a conversation with your family and find out their perspective on which principle needs work and which one interests everyone the most. Lead with curiosity. Don't make any assumptions. Ask questions directly to find out where to focus your next steps.

Remember, take small steps and give yourself the time and space to incorporate the principles. If you've never had a family meeting before, set one up in the next six months. *Schedule it.* Good things will happen! Have you already had family meetings? *Schedule the next one.* Your family is ever-changing and will benefit from formally meeting again.

If you have an advisory team, talk to them about what you learned. Get them on board. Let them know your non-financial legacy means as much to you as the legal frameworks and the performance of your investment portfolio. And find out what resources they can provide to support your family.

For more information, visit www.TheGreatestGiftBook.com for up-to-date resources, including relevant articles, tools, and adviser and facilitator referrals.

A free ebook edition is available with the purchase of this book.

To claim your free ebook edition:
1. Visit MorganJamesBOGO.com
2. Sign your name CLEARLY in the space
3. Complete the form and submit a photo of the entire copyright page
4. You or your friend can download the ebook to your preferred device

Morgan James BOGO™

A **FREE** ebook edition is available for you or a friend with the purchase of this print book.

CLEARLY SIGN YOUR NAME ABOVE

Instructions to claim your free ebook edition:
1. Visit MorganJamesBOGO.com
2. Sign your name CLEARLY in the space above
3. Complete the form and submit a photo of this entire page
4. You or your friend can download the ebook to your preferred device

Print & Digital Together Forever.

Snap a photo   Free ebook   Read anywhere

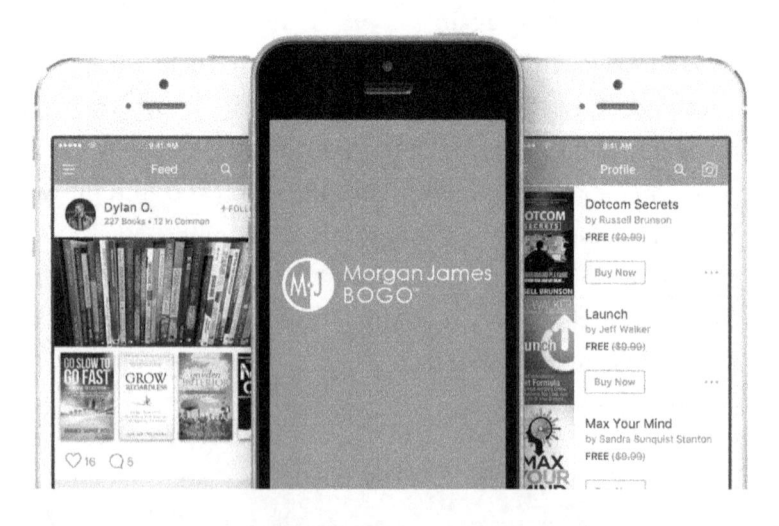